THE JAPANOPHILE'S HANDBOOK

LISTENING TO VIDEO
GAME MUSIC COVERS

JAPANESE KANJI
WRITING ON SHIRT

SHIRT WITH JAPANESE
CINEMA REFERENCE

MANGA ALWAYS IN
HAND OR NEARBY

WASABI STAINS
FROM SUSHI LUNCH

COSPLAY BOOTS OF
ANIME CHARACTER

ALEXEI MAXIM RUSSELL

THIS BOOK PUBLISHED BY
WHY NOT-WORLD DOT COM

TABLE OF CONTENTS

 The Japanophile's Handbook

TABLE OF
CONTENTS

SPECIAL THANKS

This book is published with special thanks to Misty Chronexia, The Anime Man, Sharla in Japan, Bob Samurai, Digibro, Black Critic Guy, BDUB the Anime Master, Vlad Gawron, CharlyJapan, Yuri Nakagawa and Overclocked Remix.

1.1 How to be a Japanophile

So, you want to be a Japanophile? Well, before you embark on this high and noble path, you should know that it's not for the faint of heart. It means a whole lot of research, hard work and endless hours of education, watching anime and reading Shōnen Jump. You may encounter seemingly insurmountable challenges and spine-chilling perils — such as patience-fraying encounters with the revoltingly offensive Japanopene (one who is completely ignorant of Japan) or stomach-turning brushes with the dreaded and painfully awkward Weeaboo (the wannabe Japanophile who tries way too hard). So, knowing the challenges and dangers, which lie in wait along the trail to true Japanophile enlightenment, take a moment to reflect on whether or not you have the strength, courage and persistence to walk this path with the skill and prowess of any samurai warrior.

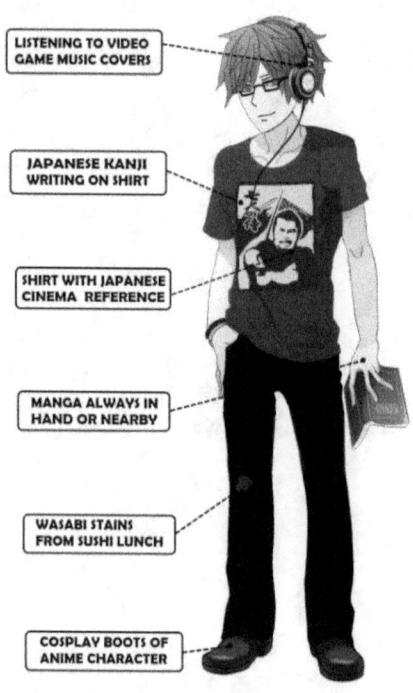

HOW TO IDENTIFY AN OTAKU

- LISTENING TO VIDEO GAME MUSIC COVERS
- JAPANESE KANJI WRITING ON SHIRT
- SHIRT WITH JAPANESE CINEMA REFERENCE
- MANGA ALWAYS IN HAND OR NEARBY
- WASABI STAINS FROM SUSHI LUNCH
- COSPLAY BOOTS OF ANIME CHARACTER

If you're still reading this, then congratulations! As the great samurai master, Musashi Miyamoto, once said "step by step, walk the thousand mile road." You'll never get anywhere unless you're willing to take that first step along the road to glory! The first thing to know is that Japanophile is not actually the preferred name for a lover of Japanese culture, nowadays. I used it for the title of this book only because everyone knows what a Japanophile is, even those who are, as yet, uninitiated and only picked up this book in order to learn and so prove themselves worthy of the title. In truth, however, if you are aspiring to become a cultured and educated connoisseur of Japanese culture then you are actually aspiring to be an Otaku, in modern language. Otaku is a Japanese word, which literally means "a young person who is obsessed with computers or particular aspects of popular culture to the detriment of their social skills." In Japan, the term has negative connotations. Meaning, pretty much, that you are at serial killer levels of social inadequacy and have a truly freakish obsession with some aspect of fandom. In Japan, there have been painfully inadequate anime-obsessed loners who have grabbed the headlines by going truly postal, in public. Lashing out and harming innocent individuals in order to vent their many frustrations. Naturally, this Japanese brand of Otakuhood is something to be avoided at all costs and is not what we're trying to encourage with this book. No, our mission, in fact, has nothing to do with this original type of Japanese Otaku. With this book, we are hoping to achieve, instead, the glorious and entirely respectable status of the adept and thoroughly uber-capable "western Otaku."

Let me tell you a story. One day, long ago, in the mists of early Internet history, a few staunch pioneers of Japanophilia appropriated the term "Otaku" in order to give a more modern and Japanese-flavored name to their great movement. Here, in the modern age, we have carried on the legacy of these great heroes by calling ourselves Otaku, in their honor. But, now that you know this, you cannot merely call yourself an Otaku because you once saw an episode of Astroboy, as a kid, and didn't mind the episode too much. No, being an Otaku requires a level of dedication and attention-to-detail worthy of the most dedicated of scientists. It's not only scientific, in its exacting standards, but is also a true art

form, insofar as it requires skill, intuition and a certain level of good taste — in the very best traditions of the authentic Japanese esthetic.

So, before you go around making a fool of yourself at the local manga comic club or revealing yourself as a total newbie on the anime forums, read the information presented to you here. So that you can walk the streets proudly in your "Akira" t-shirt, and be able to tell any passing Otaku when that anime film was created, who created it and why it helped usher in the western appreciation of manga and anime — and so prove your worthiness to call yourself an Otaku. A true Otaku would never talk about an anime/manga, or even wear such a t-shirt, unless they knew all about the series and could educate any interested or vulnerable passerby on the long and detailed history of the series and/or genre, in general. This is what it means to be a true fan and "fandom", as it's called, is an essential component of the Otaku life. Everyone who aspires to that life must acquaint themselves with it and embrace it, heart and soul.

Not only should an Otaku nurture their knowledge about anime and manga — and so water the fertile fields of fandom — they should also be conversant on all topics concerning Japan; from the importance of a particular video game franchise to the nature and significance of the Shinto torii gate. Knowing a bit of the language and being able to speak it (beyond "kawaii" and "konichiwa") will also go a long way to earning your genuine Otaku credentials.

But mostly, being an Otaku means understanding the camaraderie and soul-deep level of connection that springs into life, whenever Otaku get together to share the glorious details of their chosen fandom. This unity in fandom is a large part of the Otaku experience and the most sacred bond, to any true Otaku. Through this useful handbook, we hope to do our bit to unify and strengthen the community of Japan-loving fans that make up the Otakus of the world and so help preserve and promote the lifestyle we all love. So, forge ahead, brethren, and enjoy the sweet, creamy Japanesque goodness of the chapters ahead. By picking up this book, you've already started on the glorious path of the genuine Japanophile.

1.2 How NOT to be a Japanophile

One of the most important lessons, by far, if you want to be a true Japanophile, is learning to avoid being a mere wannabe. Whereas a modern Japanophile is referred to as an Otaku, a modern Japanophile wannabe is called a Weeaboo. "Weeaboo" is an Internet-derived conversion of the word

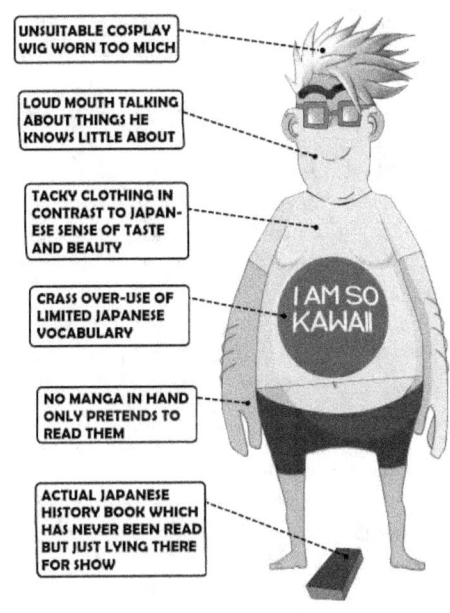

HOW TO IDENTIFY A WEEABOO

UNSUITABLE COSPLAY WIG WORN TOO MUCH

LOUD MOUTH TALKING ABOUT THINGS HE KNOWS LITTLE ABOUT

TACKY CLOTHING IN CONTRAST TO JAPANESE SENSE OF TASTE AND BEAUTY

CRASS OVER-USE OF LIMITED JAPANESE VOCABULARY

NO MANGA IN HAND ONLY PRETENDS TO READ THEM

ACTUAL JAPANESE HISTORY BOOK WHICH HAS NEVER BEEN READ BUT JUST LYING THERE FOR SHOW

I AM SO KAWAII

"Wapanese" which was once used, by western culture, to describe individuals who have such an unhealthy obsession with Japanese culture that they basically abandon their own cultures and ineptly try to pretend they are Japanese — annoying Japanese people by speaking poor Japanese and irritating their own countrymen by talking about nothing but Pocky sticks and their favorite anime episodes. The distinction between a genuine Otaku and a Weeaboo can be very difficult for the uninitiated to understand, but it is such

an important lesson for any student of Otakuhood that it is an essential distinction to make before you can proceed further.

Whereas an Otaku is a true connoisseur of the culture, showing the same reverence and respectful distance which any true expert shows to their chosen field of expertise, the Weeaboo is like a socially awkward adolescent, ineptly trying to gain the social acceptance of Japanese people — because their unfortunate mental disorder has caused them to believe they are, in fact, Japanese. Like a painfully inadequate shinobi spy, they try to disguise themselves as Japanese, attempting to walk amongst them, occasionally shouting "konichiwa!" or "kawaii!" in a pitiful attempt to blend in. Naturally, the Weeaboo is bound to fail, in this charade, and will only succeed in completely insulting the intelligence of the Japanese people and completely alienating their own friends and families, by treating them like they're from a foreign culture, completely unworthy of their respect. This type of obnoxious and desperate wannabe is something every Otaku should fear and avoid with every fiber of their being.

They are to be greatly feared, in fact, because the dark, sinister shadow of the Weeaboo dwells in us all. If you are an Otaku, or genuinely want to be one, then the shadow of the Weeaboo is like your "shadow self." It is the dark side, within you, which you must be vigilant against and fight to the finish. If you are a lover of the culture, it is tempting to become a Weeaboo. In fact, I would go as far as to say that every Otaku, at one time or another, has stepped into the fetid netherworld of Weeaboo life, during the course their Otaku careers. Simply because the fandom in your heart truly does give you an affection for the culture; the language; the people. And, until you have truly educated yourself on the actual culture, history and revered institutions of the Japanese people, you will just be a wannabee. You are, in fact, doomed to be a Weeaboo the moment you begin to love Japan. It won't be until you are fully educated and can actually claim to know and love the culture, on an intellectual level, that you can cease being a Weeaboo and graduate into even a loftier level of Otakuhood, which is so much more than just anime.

That is part of the reason why this book was created. To help Otaku, but also to help those struggling in that dark, smelly limbo of Weeaboo existence. By using the sacred knowledge of Japan, contained within the pages of this handbook, you can learn the true and factual details about the culture and so educate yourself out of the dark ignorance of Weeabooland. Carrying it at your side, like the very sword of Ichigo, you can easily dispel the sinister hollows of Weeabooland, without fear. By providing you with this guide, I am hoping I can do my bit to protect my fellow Otaku from the fate of becoming a Weeaboo or staying that way for longer than necessary.

Never give in to your dark Weeaboo impulses, but fight them at every turn. This is one of the most imperative teachings which the true Japanophile should adopt. This is because the Weeaboo life is the most certain path to failure for anyone who hopes to become a "true blue" Japanophile. The reason is simple. If you do, as you say, truly love the culture and the people then why would you wish to become the one thing all Japanese people hate the most? The Weeaboo may think, in his heart, that the Japanese should be flattered by his imitation and his desire to join their culture, but he's wrong. Very wrong. How would you feel if foreigners flooded into your country, ineptly monkeying your cultural habits, butchering your revered cultural institutions and trying to convince you they're one of you — and then becoming incensed if you get frustrated with them, tell them to go away or tell them they're making fools of themselves? You probably wouldn't be flattered at all by this invasion of pushy and desperate wannabes. In fact, you would probably harbor a secret desire to wrap your fingers around their neck and throttle them. Although they are, generally, too polite to throttle you, I assure you this is how Japanese people feel, whenever they encounter the obnoxious and overzealous Weeaboo.

In contrast, the Japanese tend to respect genuine Otaku, which they see as the legitimate non-Japanese fan-base for their many praiseworthy cultural institutions. But the operative word here is "non-Japanese." If you truly love and respect the culture and the people then do what will make them truly happy. Admire them — by all means — but as you do so, you need to fully own and retain your own nationality, at all times, and merely observe the nation of

Japan from a respectful distance. The most important lesson to learn, if you want to avoid the dark and horrible destiny of the Weeaboo can be summed up in this one simple phrase: you are not Japanese! I'm sorry to be the one to tell you this but I'm afraid it is true. You simply are NOT Japanese. No matter how many seasons of Samurai Champloo you've seen; no matter how many Kurosawa films you've watched; no matter how much you might be in love with the country and its cultural heritage — you never have been, and probably never will be, Japanese. Deal with it, because it is the single most important lesson to learn, when learning how not to be a Weeaboo. Once you have completely understood and accepted this lesson, your chances of becoming a Weeaboo plummet down to almost nil, and true, glorious Otakuhood will surely follow. This is because all Weeaboos, on some level, suffer from the delusion they're Japanese, at heart, and that all real Japanese should, therefore, accept them as such. This is the primary mental disorder, which creates the Weeaboo and which sustains their foul existence.

The second thing that defines them is ignorance. Although a Weeaboo claims to "love the culture" they usually know very little about the culture and so they are actually total frauds. They have no idea about Japan's rich history or what happened to the last samurai, Saigō Takamori. In sharp contrast to the Weeaboo, the Otakus don't dare to claim themselves connoisseurs or experts on the culture unless they are actually educated on them. They will actually go so far as to read scholarly books, watch documentaries or even visit the country in order to know what it is they're talking about. They also never suffer the delusion that they're Japanese, but rather, approach it as a passionate hobby — always looking at it from the outside in, while retaining their own cultural identity.

As a result of these commendable qualities, the fabulous and proficient Otaku often enjoys the respect and sometimes even the friendship of the Japanese people. This is because the Otaku plays it cool and doesn't make a fool of him or herself. When a Weeaboo meets a Japanese person, he gushes and gets creepy and tries too hard to impress, shouting "Arigato!" and trying to pretend they aren't foreign at all. But the Otaku, even if inwardly excited to meet

a Japanese person, shrugs it off, acts in a way appropriate to their culture, and won't make a fool of themselves by trying too hard. The Otaku understands all these ins and outs of Japanese culture and etiquette and is respectful, cool and composed at all times. As a result, Japanese people are actually more likely to like and respect them and so become their friends, even though they are not trying nearly as hard as the Weeaboo, to befriend. This casual courtesy is a fundamental key to cross-cultural communication which the Weeaboo simply does not understand. This is why they fail and why the path of the Weeaboo truly is the path of a million sorrows.

The good news, however, is that you can go a long way to avoid this horrific path simply by reading on and availing yourself of the basic education that is offered in this book. If you faithfully drink up of the sacred knowledge, contained herein, you can help assure that you are never guilty of Weeaboo ignorance and, at least, will have a rudimentary and well-rounded knowledge of the culture. It's recommended, however, that you extend your education, beyond the basic limits of this book. The more you know about the history and all other Japan-related topics — the more complete your genuine education is — the less likely it is you will ever again stray into Weeaboo territory and your future in an Otaku nirvana is assured! If you've bought this book, this should not be too much to ask — educating yourself further on all things Japanese. After all, if you're as big a Japanophile as we are then you never tire of the subject!

As a final note, there are a few powerful Japanophiles who have taken their knowledge and experience to such levels that they've actually moved to Japan and learned enough to become citizens. These heroic beings — the few, the brave, the divine — are the only exception to the Otaku rule: that you are not Japanese. Because these rarified Otaku entities are, in fact, legally Japanese. No matter their nationality, they have passed level 100, in the Otaku game and deserve full respect for their vast knowledge and mad Japan-related skillz. This is a deified level of Otakuhood we should all admire and aspire to. However, unless you have reached the level of actually being handed your Japanese passport, you must remember to always keep your Otaku cool and avoid the mistakes of the foul Weeaboo.

2.1 Anime and Manga

The first commandment of Otakuhood is a thorough knowledge of the holy scriptures — and by that, of course, I mean the full canon of manga and anime, which has been passed down to us by such prophets as "Madhouse Studio", "Bandai Entertainment" and "Shōnen Jump." Yes, knowledge of these sacred topics are one of the most essential steps to earning your Otaku stripes. In fact, the majority of us modern Otakus began our pilgrimage into full and blooming Japanophilia through the hallowed gateways of Japanese animation and comic books (known as anime and manga, respectively). And so, it is only fitting that we begin this handbook with a concise, yet thorough, education on the fundamental truths of these hallowed arts. Even if your introduction to the Japanophile lifestyle began through one of the many other gateways — such as martial arts, Japanese cinema or a keen interest in Zen Buddhism or Shinto — and so you are relatively uninitiated, about anime, it is still advisable to, at the very least, study up on anime and manga and become conversant in the genres, the history and nature of the industry, if you wish to truly walk this Earth as a bonafide Otaku. In the interest of helping you to realize that great

dream, we will now explain and outline everything you need to know, to understand the heady, wondrous world of anime and manga.

2.2 The Basics

First thing you need to know is that most popular anime series begin as a manga series. For example, the popular anime series, One Piece, which is the best-selling anime franchise in the history of the industry, began as a humble manga comic. It was first published in 1997, in serial installments, as a part of the legendary manga magazine, Weekly Shōnen Jump. Two years later, an anime, based on the manga, was produced by prominent studio, Toei Animation. It has since produced over 700 episodes, and Toei Animation has made 13 animated films, to date, based on the continuing manga series. This gives an idea about the development of most series.

The next thing you need to know is that manga and anime are classified into genres, which are outlined in the table on page 16. Many of them are self-explanatory, but some of them are unique to manga/anime and so all Otaku should study them carefully. In addition to genre divisions, manga and anime are also divided into two different types: mainstream and non-mainstream. The mainstream variety is that which is widely known and popular with the public. Non-mainstream (often called sidestream or niche) types of anime/manga are those series which are not well-known and are only popular among small niches of the population. It is the mainstream series that tend to have fandoms — often massive, and often highly opinionated, fandoms. For that reason, newbies are encouraged to study mainstream if they wish to join a community and so enjoy the support of a fandom. Niche series may well have smaller fandoms but are, characteristically, less open to new members, unless they perceive them as highly educated, concerning the intricacies of niche anime/manga. Joining a niche fandom is an expert level Otaku pursuit and so it is suggested you start with mainstream franchises. We will identify only the series with the largest fandoms, in the list below, so that new initiates to the glorious world of anime can most easily find their community,

ANIME/MANGA GENRES	DESCRIPTION
Action Adventure Comedy Drama Horror Mystery Romance Sports Fantasy Supernatural Historical Psychological Science Fiction Tragedy Martial Arts	Common, Self-explanatory genres.
Chanbara	Samurai swashbuckling genre.
Science Fantasy	A mixture of science fiction and fantasy.
Cooking	Where the story revolves around a cooking competition and the interaction of competitors.
Ecchi	Involving nudity and sexually suggestive content.
Hentai	Sexually explicit or pornographic content.
Yaoi	Is a story where a homosexual relationship between males is at the center of the story.
Yuri	Is a story where a lesbian relationship is at the center of the story.
Shoujo-ai	A non-sexually explicit version of Yuri.
Mecha	Involving pilotable robots.
Shoujo	Work that is targetted to teenaged girls.
Magical Girl	Ordinary girl using magical items to become a superhero version of themselves.
Card Battle	Involving the use of collectible card games.
Monster Battle	Centered around characters who train monsters and who engage in monster battles.
Seinen	Work targetted to older men.
Idol	Following the life story of someone who rises from obscurity to the heights of super stardom.
Slice of Life	Mundane realism or day-to-day activities.
Josei	Work that is targetted to older women.
Shounen-ai	The non-sexually explicit version of Yaoi.
Shounen	Work targetted to young boys, up to high school.
Harem	A subgenre of romance, where a male character is surrounded by female characters, who are all vying for his romantic attention.
Reverse Harem	As can be imagined, this subgenre involves a female character, surrounded by male characters, who are all vying for her romantic attention.

The Japanophile's Handbook

2.3 Beyond the Basics

Apart from the essential basics, there are other simple facts to consider before you embark on your anime adventure. Sure, you need to know the basics, as outlined above. But much like your favorite classic RPG, learning the controller instructions is only the beginning. You need the hint guide, the walkthrough, or at the very least, you need to watch the tutorial. There are certain rules and realities, within the world of anime/manga fandom, which every newcomer needs to know if they want to get past the first level boss and really get started on the road to anime Otakuhood.

For example, there is often friction between the followers of different anime. You may find flamings and accusations flying all around you, when you decide to join one fandom, simply because another fandom hates them. Even if you happen to like both anime series, you will still find yourself put into a position where you're asked to choose sides between warring fandoms. We won't mention names here, because this book is for everyone and we don't want to take sides, but your local fandom can quickly clue you in to the many feuds and trolling wars that can flare up in the anime world.

Another example of the hidden politics in the seemingly idyllic dimensions of anime fandom is the friction between mainstream and niche anime. Those who like niche anime tend to diminish the importance of mainstream anime and those who like mainstream tend to ignore the existence of niche anime. The fandoms they create, in turn, tend to be automatically opposed to each other. The mainstream faction looks upon themselves as the popular ones, helping to spread Otakuhood by welcoming newcomers and initiating them; looking upon the nichers as weebs because they're so into the more obscure, more Japan-focused anime, they seem like they think they're Japanese. The niche factions, on the other hand, see themselves as the vanguard — the true Otaku connoisseurs — whose study of the industry has surpassed the norm and so deserves a special place, a special fandom, and a status in their community. They tend to call anyone without their level of knowledge a weeb, in

spite of the fact most of them are not, simply because they have an idealistic view of Otakuhood and the level of experience which should be attained before you can assume that glorious title.

But, in reality, there is really no true metric for judging the quality of an anime series. Popularity is not necessarily an indication of quality, or lack thereof. Besides, what is popular in the west is often much different than what is popular in Japan. And so, it is all subjective, really, and, in the end, it is all a matter of personal preference. To take that point further, there is no way to judge the merit of an Otaku. Whether you're too much a purist to watch dubbed anime or have never watched anything but the big three, it is counter-productive for Otaku to judge each other too harshly. The mainstream factions do a great service to Otaku, everywhere, by welcoming in the newcomers, guiding them in the hallowed arts of fandom and priming them for a greater education, in the arcane world of niche anime. They are the true gate-keepers, through which all future Otaku start their journey, even the most learned nicher. And the nichers should be congratulated, too, for their great knowledge and their mastery of the magical arts — that being the shamanistic fervor that is true, discerning fandom. They should be respected, as well, for having the mad specialist skillz that all Otaku should attain towards. As you can see, both sides are essential to the growing movement of Otaku pride and the flowering of the community. This book is intended to help that unity, and help us to appreciate that we're all kindred spirits, united in fandom. Although differences of opinion are inevitable, we should all be on the same side, in the end, if we can ever hope to preserve our beloved culture.

Another important ethic of Otakuhood, which you need to know about, is one which spans all factions and fandoms. Namely, the duty that we all have to help "sustain the industry." This is a very important principle for the anime/manga Otaku. Sustaining the industry means buying the official DVD/Blu-ray of an anime or spending a certain portion of your income on manga or manga magazines, in order to help give a living to the people who, ultimately, keep fandom alive — the creators, the publishers and the producers. Those who help sustain the industry also help to breath

life into the entire Otaku community, by making sure the anime studios and the manga publishers stay in business, for the years and decades to come. If you're a newbie, a wannabe or do not yet understand the subtleties of the Otaku life, than you may commit the sin of watching anime streaming sites, containing pirated, illegally uploaded videos and so undermine the entire community, by threatening to bring down the publishers, screw over the creators and bring about mass bankruptcy in the anime industry. Any true Otaku, when hearing about this kind of behavior, will be negatively disposed towards you and may even eject you from their community. Doing it for a short time, because of lack of knowledge about your responsibilities, as an Otaku, may be excusable. But, once you have learned about your duty, as a dedicated disciple of fandom, it is essential that you stop at once and buy the legitimate product, unless you want to be shunned and disrespected by your brethren. If you were one of the guilty, then reading this handbook should have shown you the error of your ways. You don't need to spend a fortune on mint condition Blu-ray sets or rare, vintage manga, but you can, at least, choose legitimate video streaming services, from which the creators get a cut and which are not pirated in any way. There are many legitimate streaming sites, like this, including Crunchyroll, AnimeSuki, Hulu and even Netflix.

2.4 The Mainstream Canon

Because this book is intended as the bare-bones basics of what every Otaku (or prospective Otaku) should know, we will list only the most popular mainstream series, in order to supply you with a basic education. Those who are unfamiliar with anime and manga should start with the most well-known series, first, in order to learn the established conventions of the art and in order to find the most open fandom communities. Once you have educated yourself on these series, you can delve ever further into anime, on your own, and explore the endless depths of sidestream and niche anime. And so, here is our list of the most popular series of mainstream anime. We will start our list with three anime series that are referred to as "the big three" because they are the most commercially successful, out of all the mainstream anime.

2.4.1 The Big Three

One Piece

Manga First Published by: Shōnen Jump (weekly) serialization.
Anime Fist Produced by: Toei Animation.
Year Created: 1997.
Genre: Action, adventure, comedy, fantasy.
Description: Following the adventures of Monkey D. Luffy, One Piece is a comedic pirate adventure, set in a future time, when a world government has taken control. Pirates sail the so-called "Grand Line" of this future time, in search of the famous "One Piece" treasure. Luffy is a young, adventure-seeking 17-year-old, joined by a crew of funny and fascinating characters. This "Grand Age of Pirates" was brought about by the death of the legendary Pirate King, Gol D. Rogers. On his deathbed, he spread the rumor about the "One Piece", which is a treasure of unlimited value. This series was one of the first to become wildly popular and is still the overall best-seller of all anime/manga series. It has spawned many movies, including One Piece: The Movie, Dead End Adventure, The Giant Mechanical Soldier of Karakuri Castle and One Piece Film: Z.

Bleach

Manga First Published by: Shōnen Jump (weekly) serialization.
Anime Fist Produced by: Studio Pierrot.
Year Created: 2001.
Genre: Action, adventure, fantasy, school.
Description: The hero of this story, a young high school student named Ichigo, has the ability to see ghosts. However, his life gets even more strange and complicated when he meets a mysterious young woman named Rukia. She is a Soul Reaper, who is sent to Earth to hunt down evil, otherworldly entities called "hollows", who threaten to take over the world. During a battle with a hollow, Ichigo has some of Rukia's powers transferred onto him and becomes a Soul Reaper too. Showing a surprising amount of ability as a Soul Reaper, Ichigo soon is drawn into the battle to save the Earth.

Naruto

Manga First Published by: Shōnen Jump (weekly) serialization.
Anime Fist Produced by: Studio Pierrot.
Year Created: 1999.
Genre: Action, comedy, martial arts.
Description: A young ninja, named Naruto, lives in peaceful Hidden Leaf Village. Before being born, Naruto's village was attacked by a vicious and magical nine-tailed fox. The elder of the village, in order to save the town, allowed the fox to kill him and, using a magic hex, imprisoned the fox inside the newborn child, Naruto. Because of this curse, Naruto finds it hard to be accepted in his village and ventures out on his mission to become a village leader, meeting many interesting people along the way.

2.4.2 Mainstream Anime/Manga Series

Akame Ga Kill

Manga First Published by: Gangan Joker, serialization.
Anime Fist Produced by: White Fox Ltd.
Year Created: 2010.
Genre: Action, adventure, fantasy.
Description: This series follows the adventures of Tatsumi, a powerful fighter who is, however, none too experienced about life. When embarking on a mission to save his family from their oppressive government, Tatsumi's naivety causes him to lose all his money in a scam. Seeking to carry on in his quest, regardless, he finds himself getting mixed up with a group of assassins.

Angel Beats!

Manga First Published by: Dengeki G, serialization.
Anime Fist Produced by: P.A. Works.
Year Created: 2009.
Genre: Action, comedy, drama, school, supernatural.
Description: This story takes place in a kind of high school of the dead, but not like the famous zombie manga. This story follows the

adventures of high school student Otonashi, who has died and come to a mysterious school, which is where people go where they die. He meets another deceased girl, named Yuri, who invites him to join the "Afterlife Battlefront" or SSS, which seeks to avenge themselves on an evil god who brought misery to a lot of them, in life. The students must learn to get past their lingering attachments and unfinished business, before moving on to the next level of existence.

Anohana (The Flower We Saw that Day)

Manga First Published by: Jump SQ, serialization.
Anime Fist Produced by: A-1 Pictures.
Year Created: 2012.
Genre: Drama, slice of life, supernatural.
Description: When a young woman named Meiko dies, her five close friends begin to grow apart. One of them, Jinta, begins to abandon his life and drops out of school. Eventually becoming a shut-in, his deteriorating life soon gets a boost when the ghost of Meiko comes to him, and encourages him to fulfill a promise he made to her, when they were still children.

Another

Manga First Published by: Kadokawa Shoten, light novel.
Anime Fist Produced by: P.A.Works.
Year Created: 2009.
Genre: Horror, mystery, school, supernatural, thriller.
Description: Taking place in a school setting, this series follows the adventures of Kōichi, a new transfer student. In his new class, he always feels somewhat uneasy and freaked out by the atmosphere. However, he is soon distracted from such thoughts, when he notices a gorgeous girl named Mei, in his class. He soon discovers, however, that he's the only one who can see her.

Ao no Exorcist (Blue Exorcist)

Manga First Published by: Jump SQ, serialization.
Anime Fist Produced by: A-1 Pictures.
Year Created: 2009.
Genre: Action, demons, fantasy, shōnen, supernatural.
Description: In this series, demons and human beings live in two

adjacent worlds, which are not meant to interact. The demons live in "Gehenna" and the humans in "Assiah." In spite of the rules, the foul demons sometimes kidnap humans and bring them to Gehenna. Determined to fight back, the humans develop a class of fighters called "Exorcists." Rin, the hero, bears the curse of being a demon's illegitimate son, and yet fights the demons, as an exorcist.

Attack on Titan (Shingeki no Kyojin)

Manga First Published by: Bessatsu Shōnen, serialization.
Anime First Produced by: Production I.G/Wit Studio.
Year Created: 2009.
Genre: Action, drama, fantasy, super power, giants.
Description: This is a series about giants. Giants the size of large houses, who are extremely stupid, violent and prone to devour whole towns full of people. In this land, where giants rampage, some humans have managed to survive by enclosing themselves in a well-protected city. This story follows a young boy, named Eren, who lived about 100 years after this giant rampage. Since then, the giants have been quiet, but soon, a super giant emerges and tears down the defenses of Eren's supposedly "giant proof" home. Having been let into the city, by the super giant, smaller giants rampage through the town, killing Eren's family. Overcome with grief and rage, Eren vows to kill every single giant in the world.

Azumanga Daioh

Manga First Published by: Dengeki Daioh, serialization.
Anime First Produced by: J.C.Staff studio.
Year Created: 1999.
Genre: Comedy, slice of life, school.
Description: This story follows the lives of six schoolgirls, showcasing their amusing interactions and distinctive personalities. These girls are Chiyo (a genius), Sakaki (a shy one), Osaka (an airhead), Kagura (a jock), Tomo (a loose cannon) and Yomi (a short-tempered girl).

Bakemonogatari

Manga First Published by: Mephisto, light novel.
Anime First Produced by: Shaft studio.
Year Created: 2006.

Genre: Mystery, romance, supernatural, vampire.

Description: High school student Koyomi is a reformed vampire. Having been cured by a mysterious homeless man named Meme, Koyomi now tries to live a normal life, occasionally asking for advice from his benefactor, Meme. Along the way, he meets other people with supernatural problems, like this and tries to help them the best he can, with Meme's advice to help him.

Black Butler (Kuroshitsuji)

Manga First Published by: GFantasy, serialization.
Anime Fist Produced by: A-1 Pictures.
Year Created: 2006.
Genre: Action, black comedy, historical, dark fantasy, psychological thriller.
Description: This dark series is set in London, in the late 1800s (Victorian period). Ciel, the protagonist, has suffered a tragedy in life. His parents died in a fire and, in a moment of anger and weakness, Ciel struck a deal with a demon and sold his soul in order to get revenge for his parent's deaths. The demon he entered into this pact with becomes Ciel's butler (hence the name Black Butler) and calls himself Sebastian. Because his parents were wealthy industrialists, Ciel finds himself in charge of a massive corporation and with the help of Sebastian, manages his business, completes missions for royalty and always keeps on the watch for those responsible for his parent's deaths.

Black Lagoon

Manga First Published by: Sunday Gene-X, serialization.
Anime Fist Produced by: Madhouse studio.
Year Created: 2002.
Genre: Action, crime drama, black comedy.
Description: In this dark series, Japanese salaryman Okajima Rokuro is torn away from his life of business meetings and social drinking and karaoke parties, when he is sent to the China seas, on a business mission. However, Okajima gets kidnapped by a group of criminals, sent to thwart his mission. The gang's leader, a woman named Revy, decides to hold Okajima for ransom. However, the mysterious disc, which Okajima was told to deliver, as a part of his mission, proves to be more troublesome than any of them thought.

Blood+

Manga First Published by: Shōnen Ace, serialization.
Anime Fist Produced by: Production I.G.
Year Created: 2005.
Genre: Action, horror, adventure, science fantasy, romance, tragedy.
Description: In this series, humanity is at war with a terrifying race of monsters called Chiropterans, who are able to transform into human form. In reality, however, they are vicious monsters who live off of human blood. The human resistance, called the "Red Shield", works to track down the Chiropterans and eliminate them. The series follows the life of high school girl, Otonashi, who has no recollection of her early life. Her happy family life is eventually threatened by the realization of her ultimate fate.

Chobits

Manga First Published by: Young Magazine, serialization.
Anime Fist Produced by: Madhouse studio.
Year Created: 2000.
Genre: Romantic comedy, science fiction.
Description: Taking place in the future, Chobits is a story about Hideki, a prep school student, who wishes he could own a "Persocom" — a kind of android. Unfortunately they are very expensive and Hideki has to be satisfied with an old Persocom he finds in the trash. Naming her "Chii", he soon discovers she is far more complicated and intelligent than the average Persocom. She seems to be a more advanced android, known as a "Chobit."

Clannad

Manga First Published by: Comic Rush, serialization.
Anime Fist Produced by: Toei Animation.
Year Created: 2005.
Genre: Comedy, drama, romance, school, slice of life, supernatural.
Description: This story follows Tomoya, a young student who is disillusioned with his life. Because of several tragedies, including his mother's death in a car accident and his father's depression and alcoholism, Tomoya is a very bitter young man who has become distant from his family. After a time of this, Tomoya becomes a bit of a delinquent, getting into fights and neglecting his schoolwork. One day,

he meets a young girl named Nagisa, who is also lonely, because of having been held back a grade, due to illness. As a result she doesn't have friends in school. Through Nagisa, Tomoya catches a glimpse of a mysterious and supernatural world.

Claymore

Manga First Published by: Jump SQ, serialization.
Anime Fist Produced by: Studio Deen.
Year Created: 2001.
Genre: Dark fantasy, action, drama.
Description: Taking place in a medieval world, this world is a dangerous one. It is overrun by dangerous monsters called "youma" who can shapeshift and feed off human beings. A group of half-human/half-youma women warriors, calling themselves "The Organization" help to kill off the youma, for a fee. These female warriors are called "Claymore" because of their large claymore style swords. Only the half-breeds have enough of the youma's demonic powers to fight back. Together, a group of specialized young half-breeds team up to destroy the foul youma beasts.

Code Geass

Manga First Published by: Asaku (monthly), serialization.
Anime Fist Produced by: Bandai Entertainment/Sunrise Studio.
Year Created: 2006.
Genre: Alternate history, drama, mecha.
Description: This is a futuristic series, presenting an alternate future. This alternate universe is dominated by an empire called Britannia. They use giant robots called Knightmare Frames, to expand their empire. Japan is completely controlled by Britannia and is called "Area 11." A young man named Lelouch, living in Area 11, decides to destroy the empire. Although he is a Britannian, he promised a Japanese friend that he would try to destroy the all-powerful empire. While trying to glean military secrets of the empire, Lelouch discovers that it is a young girl, who has the power of "Geass" — which makes all people obey her will. She grants the power of Geass on Lelouch and he soon controls the Knightmare Frames and leads the rebellion against Britannia.

Cowboy Bebop

Manga First Published by: Asuka Fantasy DX, serialization.
Anime Fist Produced by: Bandai Entertainment/Sunrise studio.
Year Created: 1998.
Genre: Action, drama, science fiction, space cowboy.
Description: This futuristic cowboy series is one of the most popular series, in the west, although it enjoyed less popularity in Japan. The hero, Spike Spiegel, is a gun-slinging bounty hunter who lives from bounty to bounty, along with his posse of vagabonds: Jet Black, Valentine, Faye, Ein and Ed. Together, they hop from planet to planet, in search of riches and adventure.

Darker than Black

Manga First Published by: Asuka, serialization.
Anime Fist Produced by: Studio Deen.
Year Created: 2007.
Genre: Serial drama, action thriller, mystery, supernatural.
Description: This is a dark, complex and suspenseful series. Basically, sometime in the future, strange force-fields known as "Hell's Gate" have appeared in places such as South America and Tokyo. These strange vortexes cause a shift in the planet and cause the stars to vanish, replaced by new stars. Each of these new stars produce a race of strange, psychic citizens — with different abilities being represented by each star. These new psychic specialists become known as "contractors." The series follows Hei, a contractor who fulfills mission for the mysterious group known as the Syndicate.

Deadman Wonderland

Manga First Published by: Shōnen Ace, serialization.
Anime Fist Produced by: Manglobe studio.
Year Created: 2007.
Genre: Action, horror, science fiction.
Description: Ganta, the main character is convicted of a crime he didn't commit and is condemned to enter a new kind of correctional facility, where the inmates are forced to participate in gladiator contests. Full of dark, disturbing imagery and conspiracies, Deadman Wonderland is a good choice for those who like dark manga/anime.

Death Note

<u>Manga First Published by:</u> Shōnen Jump (weekly), serialization.
<u>Anime Fist Produced by:</u> Madhouse studio.
<u>Year Created:</u> 2003.
<u>Genre:</u> Mystery, drama, supernatural, psychological.
<u>Description:</u> A popular dark series, with psychological depth, Death Note is an original concept. In this series, there are gods of death, known as Shinigami, who can kill anyone as long as they have seen them and have written their name in a notebook called the Death Note. A Shinigami named Ryuk decides to see what would happen if a human got hold of a Death Note. He gives one to a student named Light Yagumi. The student tries to use it to improve the world, by killing off criminals, but this power goes to his head and he soon tries to establish himself as a power in the world. What's more, the death of so many criminals gets police attention and they try to track down this mysterious serial killer, who seems to target only criminals.

Dragon Ball Z

<u>Manga First Published by:</u> Shōnen Jump (weekly), serialization.
<u>Anime Fist Produced by:</u> Toei Animation.
<u>Year Created:</u> 1984.
<u>Genre:</u> Comedy, martial arts, science fantasy.
<u>Description:</u> One of the most venerable and successful series, which still has a big fanbase, Dragon Ball Z follows Goku, the protagonist, as he defends the Earth from various evil intergalactic villains. There was an original anime, simply called Dragon Ball, which chronicled the youth of Goku. Dragon Ball Z, however, follows the life of adult Goku, along with that of his son, Gohan. The story goes that Goku was originally sent down to Earth from another planet to conquer it, but lost his memory and, after interacting with earthlings, ended up defending it from all alien menaces.

Durarara!

<u>Manga First Published by:</u> ASCII Media Works, light novel.
<u>Anime Fist Produced by:</u> Brain's Base.
<u>Year Created:</u> 2004.

Genre: Action, mystery, supernatural.

Description: This series is about the exciting adventures of Ryūgamine, a country boy, in the big city. After transferring to a school in the city, he is intrigued by the various urban legends about dangers in the big city: including fighters, informants, gangs and a mysterious headless motorcycle-rider. Soon, however, he learns more than he wants to know, in the form of a supernatural gang called the "Yellow Scarves."

Elfen Lied

Manga First Published by: Weekly Young Jump, serialization.

Anime Fist Produced by: Arms Corporation.

Year Created: 2002.

Genre: Psychological horror, romance, science fantasy.

Description: In this series, a mutated strain of human, called "The Diclonius", has mysterious psychic powers and telekinetic abilities. One of them, Lucy, has been captured in a laboratory, for study. However, it is soon discovered this particular Diclonius is dangerously psychotic and homicidal. She breaks free of the laboratory, leaving bloody corpses in her wake, until she makes good her escape. After an accidental fall, however, she is lost in the ocean. She ends up washed on a distant shore, with no memory of the past. Two teens, Yuka and Kouta, find her and befriend her — taking her into their home. Soon, however, the true nature of the Diclonius shines through.

Fairy Tail

Manga First Published by: Shōnen Magazine, serialization.

Anime Fist Produced by: A-1 Pictures.

Year Created: 2006.

Genre: Action, adventure, magic, fantasy, comedy, ecchi.

Description: This series takes place in a supposedly imaginary world called "The Earth Land" (huh?). But, anyways, this apparently mythical land is renowned for its mage guild, which is known as "Fairy Tail." The young heroine, Lucy Heartfilia, wishes to join this illustrious school. She embarks on a journey to fulfill her mission and meets a boy named Natsu. Little does she know, however, that Natsu is a mage of the Fairy Tail guild.

Fate / Stay Night

Manga First Published by: Shōnen Ace, serialization.
Anime Fist Produced by: Studio Deen.
Year Created: 2005.
Genre: Action, romance, contemporary fantasy.
Description: This is basically a magic battle series. The hero, Shirou, was brought up by a powerful wizard, after his parents came to a tragic end. Using his rudimentary magic skills, Shirou tries to help people and make good use of his powers. Eventually, he gets mixed up in a magic battle that is far outside of his magical abilities and, in the heat of the fray, he unlocks some incredible magical abilities he never knew he had. Having miraculously summoned a great protector, named Saber, this graduation into the realms of higher magic comes with a price. He is drawn into a ruthless magical battle known as the "Holy Grail War" and must augment his magic skills fast if he has any hope of competing in this high level battle!

Food Wars (Shokugeki no Souma)

Manga First Published by: Shōnen Jump (weekly), serialization.
Anime Fist Produced by: J.C. Staff.
Year Created: 2012.
Genre: Cooking, Ecchi, School.
Description: Our personal favorite, as far as Cooking genre series go, this series follows the life of Suoma, who is the son of a famous chef. Having worked in his dad's restaurant, Suoma is eventually sent to the high profile culinary school known as Tootsuki Culinary Academy. There, very few students are good enough to graduate and must pit their skills against each other in ruthless "Shokugeki" or "food wars" competitions. The series follows his education and his interaction with the other students of the academy.

FLCL

Manga First Published by: Magazine Z, serialization.
Anime Fist Produced by: Manglobe Inc.
Year Created: 1999.
Genre: Action, comedy-drama, science fiction.

Description: This is a light-hearted series, revolving around Naota, a twelve year-old boy, who gets hit by a space ship, piloted by a girl named Haruko. Soon afterwards, he finds she has joined his household, as a servant, and is, in fact, an extraterrestrial investigator on a mission.

Fruits Basket

Manga First Published by: Hana to Yume, serialization.
Anime Fist Produced by: Studio Deen.
Year Created: 1998.
Genre: Fantasy, drama, romantic comedy, reverse harem.
Description: This might be the most popular Reverse Harem out there. Tooru, the protagonist, is an orphaned 16 year-old. She is invited to join the household of a boy named Yuki and his cousins, Shigure and Kyou. Unknown to Tooru, however, this family is cursed. They transform into animals if they embrace a member of the opposite sex. Tooru gets to know the family better (particularly the boys) and the dark shadow of the family curse causes drama and heartbreak.

Full Metal Alchemist

Manga First Published by: Shōnen Gangan, serialization.
Anime Fist Produced by: Bones studio.
Year Created: 2001.
Genre: Adventure, drama, fantasy.
Description: This series had a large and loyal fandom when it first came out and is still wildly popular. It is set in an interesting, almost steam punk universe, similar to the European industrial revolution times. It follows two brothers, Edward and Alphonse, who have tried to bring their dead mother back to life, using the forbidden science of "Alchemy." However, as a result, they lose parts of their own bodies. Ed loses his leg and Al's soul ends up being sealed in a huge suit of armor. Growing in skill, as an alchemist, Ed eventually becomes a nationally certified alchemist and so becomes known as the "Full Metal Alchemist." The brothers search for the "Philosopher's Stone", an alchemical artifact that would allow them to regain their normal human bodies.

Full Metal Panic!

Manga First Published by. Newtype, serialization.

Anime Fist Produced by: Gonzo studio.
Year Created: 2003.
Genre: Action, comedy, drama, sci-fi.
Description: The protagonist, Sousuke, is a young military specialist working for a top secret anti-terrorist organization. His latest mission is to protect a young schoolgirl, named Kaname, who is being targeted by terrorist organizations. Kaname, however, is blissfully unaware. Sousuke joins her school, in order to keep tabs on her, but soon sticks out like a sore thumb, for his cold, military views on life, and his complete lack of social experience. Sousuke forms a bond with Kaname and she soon realizes that he is there to protect her from forces she never knew existed.

Future Diary (Mirai Nikki)

Manga First Published by: Dengeki G, serialization.
Anime Fist Produced by: P.A. Works.
Year Created: 2009.
Genre: Action, comedy, drama, school, supernatural.
Description: This is a supernatural school series. Amano is a schoolboy who feels ignored by the world. He can't make friends easily and lives the life of a loner. His only confidante is his cell phone diary, where he confides his private thoughts and his disappointments. In his solitude, he invents an imaginary friend, who has supernatural powers and can control reality. This friend, named Deus Ex Machina, gives Amano the power to change his life. With Deus' help, Amano can now create his future, simply by writing it in his cell phone diary.

Guilty Crown

Manga First Published by: Shōnen Gangan, serialization.
Anime Fist Produced by: Production I.G.
Year Created: 2011.
Genre: Action, drama, science fiction, shōnen, super power.
Description: An apocalyptic series, this follows the adventures of Shu, who has lost his entire family to a deadly epidemic, brought to Earth by a meteorite. Shu has become a despondent and weak person, after his loss, but is soon brought back to life when he meets a stunning pop idol, named Inori. It turns out that Inori has a secret weapon, and is being pursued by a government agency, which is after her powers. As the head of the rebellion, against this agency, Inori grants her secret

powers onto Shu. Shu has to make the choice if he wants to join the rebellion and help rebuild the world.

Gurren Lagann

Manga First Published by: Dengeki Daioh, serialization.
Anime Fist Produced by: Gainax co.
Year Created: 2007.
Genre: Action, adventure, comedy-drama, mecha.
Description: In the future, humans are forced to live in underground cities by a despotic ruler, Lordgenome. Simon and Kamina vow to find a way to return to the surface. Using their skills as underground drillers, they eventually succeed and find the humans that remain on the surface face all kinds of daily perils, led by Lordgenome. Simon and Kamina then embark on a mission to topple the evil overworld dictator.

Hellsing

Manga First Published by: Young King OURs, serialization.
Anime Fist Produced by: Gonzo KK.
Year Created: 1997.
Genre: Action, drama, horror, science fantasy.
Description: In England, supernatural threats and vampires are fought off by the Hellsing Organization. Alucard, a vampire who has entered into a pact to serve the Hellsing, is the main character. Through her and Hellsing's crime and vampire fighting adventures, they soon discover a new and even more sinister force rising in England.

High School DxD

Manga First Published by: Light novel.
Anime Fist Produced by: TNK studio.
Year Created: 2008.
Genre: Comedy, demons, ecchi, fantasy, romance, school, harem.
Description: A dark harem series, Issei, the protagonist really wants to have a harem of girls. Unfortunately, his dating career takes a nosedive when he dates a girl who is actually a vicious demon. She brutally kills him and then ensnares his soul, forcing him to reincarnate into her demonic realm and so become her slave.

High School of the Dead

Manga First Published by: Dragon Age, serialization.
Anime Fist Produced by: Madhouse studio.
Year Created: 2006.
Genre: Action, ecchi, horror, supernatural.
Description: A very popular horror echhi, HOTD takes place in a high school zombie apocalypse setting. Takashi, the hero, is a student in a school which has an infectious outbreak, causing people to turn into zombies. With the help of his friends and school staff, they try to fight off the zombie hordes, while simultaneously trying to discover what caused the mysterious epidemic.

Inuyasha

Manga First Published by: Shōnen Sunday, serialization.
Anime Fist Produced by: Bandai Entertainment/Sunrise studio.
Year Created: 1996.
Genre: Action, romance, supernatural.
Description: This series has its dedicated fandoms. It takes place in the Sengoku period of feudal Japan. It follows the adventures of Kagome, who is pulled into a well and finds herself transported to this historical era of Japan. It turns out she was pulled into this world by demons who want a powerful jewel that was inside Kagome's body. And, what's worse, the demons are now after her. She enlists the help of a friend named Inu Yasha (a half demon), in order to ward off the demons and prevent them from wielding its power.

Kill la Kill

Manga First Published by: Young Ace, serialization.
Anime Fist Produced by: Studio Trigger.
Year Created: 2013.
Genre: Action, comedy, school, magical girl.
Description: A magical girl series, it follows Ryuko, a girl looking for the people who killed her father. This puts her into conflict with various enemies, including the student council president Satsuki (a bit of dictator) and her mother's powerful fashion empire. Ryuko is distinctive for wielding a blade that looks like half of a pair of huge, broken scissors.

K-on

Manga First Published by: Manga Time Kirara, serialization.
Anime Fist Produced by: Kyoto Animation.
Year Created: 2007.
Genre: Comedy, music, school, slice of life.
Description: A slice of life series, it is about Yui, a schoolgirl who is looking for a social group. She wants to join a club of some kind and soon finds a light music club, headed by drummer Ritsu and Yui's friend, bassist Mio. The club is about to be defunded because of low membership. Desperately working to save it, they manage to fill all spots except one. Yui ends up playing the guitar and proves to be much more talented than any of them ever imagined.

Mahou Shoujo Madoka ★ Magica

Manga First Published by: Nitroplus Books, light novel.
Anime Fist Produced by: Shaft studio.
Year Created: 2011.
Genre: Drama, magic, psychological, thriller.
Description: Another good Magical Girl series, this series is about Madoka, who takes notice of a new and mysterious classmate. She seems to recognize this girl from a dream — a dream where a cat-like being addresses her, offering her a higher destiny. Later, she finds this mystery girl fighting with this same cat-like thing and she is asked, again, if she'd like to embrace a higher destiny, but this time in real life. Is she willing to become a magical girl and accept the consequences and the responsibilities this entails?

Melancholy of Haruhi Suzumiya

Manga First Published by: The Sneaker, serialization.
Anime Fist Produced by: Kyoto Animation.
Year Created: 2003.
Genre: Comedy, romance, sci-fi, psychological.
Description: A strange and interesting series about Haruhi, a young student who tells everyone that she has no interest in ordinary humans, but is very interested in psychics, espers, time travelers and aliens. She asks for all people who fall into these categories to join her. Everyone ignores her and considers her very strange, except for Kyon, who is the only one who talks to her. After noticing that she can't find a decent

club to join, Haruhi gets the idea to gather together the school into her own group, which, with predictable weirdness, she calls "Save our World by Overloading it with Fun Suzumiya Haruhi Brigade" (or S.O.S. Brigade).

Mushi-Shi

Manga First Published by: Afternoon Seasons Zōkan, serialization.
Anime Fist Produced by: Artland Inc.
Year Created: 1999.
Genre: Action, drama, horror, science fantasy.
Description: In a fictional era of Japanese history, where 19th century technology exists, but Japan is still closed off from the rest of the world, there are mysterious people called "Mushi-shi." These spiritual individuals can interact with the "Mushi" who are an ethereal form of primal spirit being, which cannot be perceived by most people. Ginko, the hero, is one of them and we follow him as he uses his "Mushi whisperer" type powers to solve various supernatural powers, among the populace.

Neon Genesis Evangelion

Manga First Published by: Shōnen Ace, serialization.
Anime Fist Produced by: Gainax co.
Year Created: 1994.
Genre: Post-apocalyptic, mecha.
Description: In the future, in a place called Neo Tokyo-3, Shinji is summoned to take part in a giant robot battle. Summoned by his father, he is asked to take control of a giant robot called EVA01 and so protect the world, which is under attack. These enemies, known as "angels", are apparently hostile, but Shinji, being estranged from his cold father, has doubts about them and the intentions of his father, making him wonder if he should take the mission.

No Game No Life

Manga First Published by: MF Bunko J, light novel.
Anime Fist Produced by: Madhouse studio.
Year Created: 2012.
Genre: Adventure, comedy, ecchi, fantasy, game, supernatural.
Description: A quality Game genre series, No Game No Life follows the adventures of Shiro and Sora, step-siblings, who own the famous

online gaming handle "Blank" — which is renowned for never having been defeated. However, when they're invited to a chess match, they find themselves getting more than they bargained for, when Tet, the God of Games, challenges them.

Noragami

<u>Manga First Published by:</u> Monthly Shōnen Magazine, serialization.
<u>Anime Fist Produced by:</u> Bones studio.
<u>Year Created:</u> 2010.
<u>Genre:</u> Action, comedy, supernatural.
<u>Description:</u> An interesting Supernatural Comedy series, it is about an inconsequential little god, named Yato, who is frustrated that no one has created even one single shrine, in his honor. In the hopes of fixing this sad situation, he scrawls his name on a bathroom wall, downtown, advertizing himself as the "delivery god", who will deliver his divine aid, in exchange for a simple offering to him, as a deity. Hiyori, a young girl, is soon rescued by Yato, and together with another boy, Yukine, they join Yato on an adventure where his origins and hidden history is revealed to him, at last.

One Punch Man

<u>Manga First Published by:</u> Tonari no Young Jump, serialization.
<u>Anime Fist Produced by:</u> Madhouse studio.
<u>Year Created:</u> 2012.
<u>Genre:</u> Action, comedy.

<u>Description:</u> This series is wildly popular in Japan. Although, at the time of publication, it hadn't yet reached as much popularity in the west, its following is already growing and we forecast it will be extremely popular, in no time. Saitama, the hero, has a hidden super power — he can defeat any enemy in one punch. The series follows his hilarious adventures as he tries to find an enemy worthy enough to stand up to his all-powerful fist!

Ouran High School Host Club

<u>Manga First Published by:</u> LaLa Magazine, serialization.
<u>Anime Fist Produced by:</u> Bones studio.

Year Created: 2006.
Genre: Drama, harem, romantic comedy.
Description: A kind of gender-bender Harem genre series, which is, nevertheless, very popular. The main character is named Harumi. Being a new student, in a posh private school, she is looking for a club to join, in order to make friends. She soon finds herself a member of the "Host Club" which is designed for gorgeous young men to entertain ladies. Sadly, for Harumi, she has been mistaken for a guy and so needs to keep up the charade and entertain the enthusiastic ladies of the club!

Psycho-Pass

Manga First Published by: Jump SQ, serialization.
Anime Fist Produced by: Production I.G.
Year Created: 2012.
Genre: Action, police, psychological, science fiction.
Description: In this dark, technological police series, law enforcement has attained the technology to predict crime, by instantly measuring a person's state of mind. If they're close to committing a crime, these police of the future endeavor to stop them, before the fact. Those who are analyzed are said to be "Psycho-Passed." The hero, Shinya, is an officer who uses this technology to fight crime, in this future society.

Rurouni Kenshin (Samurai X)

Manga First Published by: Shōnen Jump (weekly), serialization.
Anime Fist Produced by: Studio Gallop/Studio Deen.
Year Created: 1994.
Genre: Chanbara, action, adventure.
Description: This series is one of the legendary pioneers of quality chanbara manga. The hero, Kenshin, is an extremely strong rurouni warrior, who was once an assassin, during the Japanese historical epoch of the Meiji restoration. Taking place in the Meiji era, his adventures lead him to a kendo school, where he makes a few friends, including a female Kendo master, a former thief and a doctor. With their help, Kenshin has to face the ghosts of his past, as well of those of his new-found friends.

Samurai Champloo

Manga First Published by: Shōnen Ace, serialization.

<u>Anime Fist Produced by:</u> Manglobe Inc.

<u>Year Created:</u> 2004.

<u>Genre:</u> Action, adventure, chanbara, comedy-drama.

<u>Description:</u> Another highly popular series, this takes place in feudal Japan and follows the adventures of three friends (well, sort of): Mugen, a rough, ill-mannered vagabond, who can, nonetheless, really kick ass; Jin, an unemployed samurai who lives by the honorable code of the samurai, and can also kick ass, in his noble, traditional Kendo kind of way; and Fuu, a young, somewhat ditzy girl who has brought them all together, on a mission to find the mysterious "samurai who smells of sunflowers." Full of quality comedy, artistry and historical references, it's one of our personal favorites.

Soul Eater

<u>Manga First Published by:</u> Shōnen Gangan, serialization.

<u>Anime Fist Produced by:</u> Bones studio.

<u>Year Created:</u> 2003.

<u>Genre:</u> Action, adventure, black comedy, fantasy, supernatural.

<u>Description:</u> This is a dark supernatural combat series, which features a kind of secret gladiator school, run by the death spirit, Shinigami. Hidden deep in the state of Nevada, USA, this school features individuals who can transform into weapons. The people who then wield these living weapons are called "Weapon Meisters." The competitors of this school compete to create the ultimate living weapon, called the "Death Scythe." This weapon can be wielded by Shinigami. In order to create a death scythe, the living weapon needs to defeat and devour the soul of 99 evil humans and 1 witch.

Sword Art Online

<u>Manga First Published by:</u> Dengeki Bunko, serialization.

<u>Anime Fist Produced by:</u> A-1 Pictures.

<u>Year Created:</u> 2012.

<u>Genre:</u> Action, adventure, science fiction, game.

<u>Description:</u> Perhaps the most popular Game genre series, SAO is about virtual reality and multi-player online gaming, in the future. Based in 2022, it originally spawned from a series of light novels, telling many different stories. But, basically, it involves a new form of virtual reality, where the players don't use controllers or keyboards, but control their online characters with their bodies and brain. Because their senses are

locked into the game, pain and death in the game can translate into the real world, creating a high-stakes and perfectly realistic alternate universe, where players battle it out and embark on adventures together, as well as facing real-world perils, such as getting stuck in the game and beta-testing as yet unexplored VR worlds. This is a high quality choice for serious gamers.

Tokyo Ghoul

Manga First Published by: Young Jump, serialization.
Anime Fist Produced by: Studio Pierrot.
Year Created: 2011.
Genre: Action, drama, horror, mystery, psychological, seinen, supernatural.
Description: Ken, the protagonist of this story, is a kind of geeky guy. Eventually, however, he meets a girl named Rize and they seem to click. Having the same interests and being the same age, they eventually grow close. However, Ken soon discovers that Rize is actually a "ghoul," a kind of monster that lives off human flesh. Ken soon becomes a ghoul himself and becomes trapped in Rize's dark world, where humans are the prey.

Toradora!

Manga First Published by: Dengeki Daioh, serialization.
Anime Fist Produced by: J.C. Staff.
Year Created: 2006.
Genre: Drama, romantic comedy.
Description: This is a romantic comedy series following the adventures of the hero, Ryuji, as he tries to get a girlfriend. He is happy to be put in the same class as his crush, pretty schoolgirl Minoru. But he is soon thwarted when Minoru's vicious and tempermental friend, Taiga, takes a disliking to him and gets between them. However, learning Taiga has a crush on his best friend, Ryuji makes a deal with her, for them to cooperate and so get both their crushes. As a result of this cooperation, however, it soon becomes rumored that Ryuji and Taiga seem to be spending too much time together and they both come to the awkward realization that they've become close.

2.5 The Western Pioneers of Anime

In addition to the modern mainstream canon, all Otaku should be aware of the early history of anime, and how it came to be known, and loved, in the west. As strange as it may seem to the modern-day Otaku, there was a time when Japanese animation was, literally, unknown outside of Japan. I call this dark period of the olden days "The Dark Ages" (not to be confused with the epoch of European history, which goes by the same name).

Basically, it was only a handful of anime series which, together, helped to pioneer the popular acceptance of anime, in the west, and so created the vast nation of Otakus which now exist. The first, and most significance, was the venerable anime series Astro Boy (also called Tetsuwan Atom, or "Mighty Atom" in Japan). Although the Astro Boy manga had existed since 1952 — the invention of legendary manga pioneer Osamu Tezuka — it wasn't until 1963 that it was made into an anime, by Mushi Production studio (or Mushi Pro). This was, probably, the very first series to follow the manga-to-anime formula and really did a lot to pioneer this tradition, which still is going strong today. And even this early broadcast of the quaint, black and white 1960s anime on NBC television network, in the United States, didn't succeed in converting the west to full Otakuhood. It took a long time and multiple exposures to the glories of anime before the west came to their senses, took notice and came to fully appreciate what they were viewing.

It really wasn't until the 1980s, when Astro Boy was rebooted in a slicker, more modern, well-scored and full-color format, that the west began to sit up and take notice, and so the seeds of Otakuhood were planted in the minds of a generation of children. Astro Boy, although not popular with Otakus, today, really was a pioneering force in the creation of modern anime and manga, both in the west and in Japan. Although, this series, alone, didn't launch the movement. It was the simultaneous emergence of a great many popular Japanese series, all coming together in the 1980s, which really gave birth to the Otaku movement. There was the

launch of RoboTech, in the 1980s. The first popular Mecha anime, this series was created for the US market — having been created from out of the stories of numerous Mecha manga, all thrown together, into a single compelling story. This series brought exciting anime into the lives of millions of western children, at the same time that Astro Boy was becoming popular. Along with the creation of multiple full-length films, all through the 1980s, this really helped to spark the first flames of anime fandom, in the west.

The release of the iconic film, Akira, based on the legendary cyberpunk manga series, by Katsuhiro Otomo, was the first truly popular anime film to appeal to adults, in the west. It helped spark the western interest in manga which, up to then, had been virtually non-existent. The films of Hayao Miyazaki, the most revered of early anime film directors, also emerged at the same time and really helped to cement the legitimacy of the anime film, in the minds of the west, with such critical and commercial successes as Nausicaä of the Valley of the Wind and My Neighbour Totoro.

The 1990s and early 2000s saw the expansion of "anime mania" continuing, unfettered, with even greater successes by Hayao Miyazaki, through such legendary films as Princess Mononoke and Spirited Away. The now iconic film, Ghost in the Shell, brought the most modern and compelling version of psychological cyberpunk, since Akira, introduced Ecchi to the west and served as the inspiration for the film The Matrix — demonstrating just how legitimate anime had come to be seen, in the eyes of Hollywood. Such anime series, for children, as Pokemon, Digimon and Sailor Moon continued the Otaku-friendly rearing of yet another generation of children — deepening and solidifying the grip of anime-appreciation, until it has reached the level of cohesion and power, which it now enjoys today. All true Otaku should know this history, at least to the degree it is outlined, in this book. Although further study, outside the limits of this work, is greatly recommended. In the interest of providing that compulsory level of education, we'll now list the details of all the pioneering anime works, in chronological order. In addition to a few more modern

films which are, I think, destined to become a part of the ever-evolving history of anime.

Astro Boy (Tetsuwan Atom)

Manga First Published by: Kobunsha publishing.
Anime Fist Produced by: Mushi Production.
Year Created: 1952.
Genre: Action, adventure, mecha, sci-fi.
Description: Set in the (supposedly) distant year of 2003, Astro Boy is a Sci-fi series, where robots have become a major part of life on Earth. After his son dies, a robotic scientist creates a robot boy to replace him. Named Tobio, this robot fails to satisfy the scientist and he throws Tobio into the scrap heap. Later, Tobio is rescued by a prominent crusader for "robot rights", named Professor Ochanomizu. The professor renames him Astro Boy and discovers his many super powers. Given his great powers, Astro Boy is soon enlisted to help defend the Earth from a variety of villains. By helping the world, Astro Boy attempts to teach the world about robot rights, by showing that robots, like him, do good deeds for the planet.

Nausicaä of the Valley of the Wind

Director: Hayao Miyazaki.
Year Created: 1984.
Genre: Adventure, drama, fantasy, post-apocalyptic.
Description: This is the first popular film by legendary director, Hayao Miyazaki. The main character, Princess Nausicaä, lives in the peaceful Valley of the Wind. Sadly, her kingdom has been overrun by poisonous mushrooms and the threat of their warlike neighbours. But the princess soon proves to have latent, unrealized potential and just might possess the power to save her land and its people.

RoboTech

Anime Fist Produced by: Tatsunoko Productions.
Year Created: 1985.
Genre: Mecha, action, adventure, sci-fi, mystery, romance.
Description: This film was actually made out of three unrelated anime, pieced together for the American market. In spite of this, it still

produced a high quality series, which was legendary as a pioneer, leading to anime's greater popularity. It also spawned several movies, novels, role playing games, toys and video games. In fact, RoboTech games are still being made. Most recently, "RoboTech: Invasion" (2004) for Xbox and PS2. The story of the anime is long and complex (as can be expected from such a pieced-together anime), but basically involves the adventures of pilots, operating massive mecha robots. This advance robot technology was created from alien technology, discovered by humanity when an alien craft crashed into Earth. The creators of these big robots then used the alien's own technology to fight off a series of extra-terrestrial invasions.

Castle in the Sky

Director: Hayao Miyazaki.
Year Created: 1986.
Genre: Action, drama, fantasy, sci-fi.
Description: The second popular film by Hayao Miyazaki, this one involves a flying city. In the story, humans lived in flying cities, in the distant past. But most had lowered down to the Earth and only one remains in the sky. The heroine, Sheeta, after falling from an airship, embarks on a dangerous adventure with her new friend, Pazu. The chase leads them to this last remaining floating city, where they learn about an ancient race of people.

Akira

Director: Katsuhiro Otomo.
Year Created: 1988.
Genre: Action, horror, psychological, sci-fi, post-apocalyptic, political thriller, cyberpunk.
Description: Like a lot of the Sci-fi genre anime of the early days, this "future" world of 2019, is a bit off, as far as predicting the future. But regardless, Akira is one of the true break-out works of anime that helped bring the genre to the west and it's a legendary work of artistry. In the world of Akira, the main character, Tetsuo, lives in a post-apocalyptic world, decimated by World War III. In Neo-Tokyo, where he lives, the underworld is practically in charge and the legal authorities can barely manage to stop them from gaining complete and permanent control. Tetsuo gains psychic powers, through involvement in a

government experiment and begins to use his powers to get revenge on the world, which he feels has wronged him.

My Neighbour Totoro

Director: Hayao Miyazaki.
Year Created: 1988.
Genre: Adventure, comedy, supernatural.
Description: The third great film by Hayao Miyazaki, this is set in post-war, rural Japan. It is a tale of two girls, whose mother is in the hospital. Feeling lonely, the girls explore a large tree in their yard and discover it contains three supernatural beings of the forest (called Totoros). When their mother can't return to them and one of the girls runs away, in search of their mother, the other sister petitions the Totoros to help them.

Sailor Moon

Manga First Published by: Nakayoshi, serialization.
Anime Fist Produced by: Toei Animation.
Year Created: 1991.
Genre: Action, comedy, drama, magical girl, romance.
Description: The original Magical Girl genre series, this is one who helped define the genre and is probably the most popular. It follows the adventures of Usagi (called Serena in the English version), a somewhat ditzy and hyperactive schoolgirl. One day, she meets a talking cat named Luna and learns that she has untapped powers, which she must use to combat a dark empire called the "Negaverse" or "Dark Universe", which is run by the evil Queen Beryl and her endless procession of generals, all named after metals. And so, Usagi is reborn as the super hero, Sailor Moon. Usagi meets other girls, who she discovers are also part of her super hero group. Together, the group of heroes fight an epic battle with Queen Beryl and the Negaverse.

Ghost in the Shell

Director: Mamoru Oshii.
Year Created: 1995.
Genre: Action, psychological, sci-fi, cyberpunk.
Description: Another iconic work, the original Ghost in the Shell is still a thriving series, with "Ghost in the Shell: Arise" being released in 2015.

This original film invented the particular genre of cyberpunk involving cyborgs and humans in robotic bodies and helped inspire the creation of the film, "The Matrix". The original movie was set in 2029. In this future, cybernetics has reached such a point, that humans are no longer limited to flesh and can be improved with cybernetic limbs or have their "ghosts" or spirits put into new, robotic shells. This gives birth to a new phenomenon, though, where hackers can break into people's bodies and gain control, wreaking havoc. The story follows the adventures of a group of cybernetically-enhanced law enforcement officers, who are tasked to track down these hackers.

Princess Mononoke

Director: Hayao Miyazaki.
Year Created: 1997.
Genre: Adventure, drama, fantasy.
Description: Another famous work by Hayao Miyazaki, this one takes place in medieval Japan. The main character, Ashitaka, has been forced to battle with a demon and, in the process of dispatching him, has been cursed. Hoping to find a cure, he ventures into a forest full of nature spirits and deities, with magical powers. There, he finds there is a war going on between the forest gods and the Lady Eboshi, who is the leader of a nearby village.

Pokemon

Anime Fist Produced by: OLM, inc.
Year Created: 1997.
Genre: Action, adventure, comedy, fantasy, kids.
Description: This is a staple of many a childhood and probably a first contact with anime, for a lot of kids. Pokemon, unlike most anime, was spawned from two Nintendo Gameboy games called "Pokemon Red" and "Pokemon Blue." It is still extremely popular with kids, today. In this series, a boy named Satoshi is interested in training monsters, for battle. This kind of trainer is known as a "Pokemon Master." He soon finds a monster to train, in the form of a cute yellow creature named Pikachu. Satoshi is soon joined by new friends, Takeshi and Kasumi, and together they aspire to join the famous monster battle competitions.

Digimon

Anime Fist Produced by: Toei Animation.

Year Created: 1999.

Genre: Action, adventure, monster battle, comedy, fantasy, kids.

Description: This is another staple of childhood, for a lot of future Otaku! In this series, we follow main character Tai, who is transported to the "Digital World" and meets various "digital monsters." He also meets a group of other kids, who have been transported to this world with him. Each kid soon finds a special monster, assigned to them, which they can train and so bring out their true potential. Successful training causes each kid's monster to "digivolve" into a more powerful monster. These kids soon learn they are a "chosen group" destined to save the digital world. Together, they must use their training skills to digivolve their monsters into fighters strong enough to conquer the evil monsters, which threaten to take over the Digital World.

Spirited Away

Director: Hayao Miyazaki.

Year Created: 2001.

Genre: Fantasy.

Description: This film by Hayao Miyazaki is about a little girl named Chihiro and her family. On their way to a new home, they find an abandoned theme park. Unfortunately, this is actually a playground for the gods and not intended for humans, at all. Chihiro and her family are punished for trespassing on this theme park and Chihiro, on her own, needs to figure out how to rescue herself and her parents.

Howl's Moving Castle

Director: Hayao Miyazaki.

Year Created: 2004.

Genre: Adventure, drama, fantasy, romance.

Description: This Hayao Miyazaki film is actually based on a novel by a British author, Diana Wynne Jones. In it, a girl named Sophie is transformed into an old woman. Understandably distraught, she wanders away from her home, in search of a cure for her affliction. Eventually she helps the servant of a powerful and feared wizard named Howl. By befriending Howl and his dark, magical friends, she hopes to find a way to restore her lost youth.

The Girl Who Leapt Through Time

Director: Mamoru Hosoda.
Year Created: 2006.
Genre: Adventure, comedy, drama, romance, sci-fi.
Description: This recent film is not a classic of anime, but is destined to become one, in our opinion. It follows the life of Makoto, who has the power to travel through time. She uses this power to improve her life, in various small ways, but soon discovers there are serious consequences to her actions and she tries to wield her power in such a way to better shape her future and those of her loved ones.

5 Centimeters Per Second

Director: Makoto Shinkai.
Year Created: 2007.
Genre: Drama, romance.
Description: This fascinating romantic film is set in Japan, from 1990 to 2007, and follows the life of a young boy named Takaki. Consisting of three acts, the first one starts in 1990, before the Internet had emerged. Two young people form a strong bond, in school, writing letters to each other, in friendship. At last, their feelings culminate in a kiss, but they are forced to separate, soon after, promising to write. In future acts, email becomes a part of the story, when the man is seen writing endless emails, which it is later discovered, are written to his old flame, who he has lost touch with. In spite of the fact he can't send these emails, he writes them to ease his heart. In the end, they are living separate lives — with the boy employed as a computer programmer and the girl about to get married. But he ends up losing his job and spiraling out of control, because of memories of his lost love and she, finding his old letters, also doubts her marriage. And then, after 17 years, fate brings the two together, again, by chance.

3.1 Japanese Cinema

If you don't know who Takeshi Kitano is or if you don't know who played the lead in Kurosawa's "Yojimbo" then your Otaku credentials are, indeed, in question. Although the first commandment may have everything to do with anime knowledge, this is also where so many Japanophiles go wrong and are lead astray onto the wayward path of the Weeaboo. For, it is written, that if any Japanophile's knowledge of Japan does not extend beyond the confines of anime and manga then said Japanophile is, in fact, a Weeaboo. In order to avoid that fate, it is absolutely essential to know more about Japan than what is available to you, in the world of anime. If you truly want to be called a Japanophile, you need a wide range of knowledge about every significant subject which relates to Japan. Anyone with a one-sided view of Japan is not a true Japanophile. I don't care if you've memorized the story arcs of all sixteen seasons of Bleach, you will still not have earned your Otaku badge, unless you can balance off that expert knowledge with a reasonable amount of familiarity with other Japanese subjects, such as customs, culture or cinema.

This is the second commandment of Otakuhood. You must have a range of knowledge, in order to be a full Otaku. Anime, alone, is not enough. Nothing annoys the Japanese more than an anime/manga fan who is so steeped in the fandom that they move to Tokyo, rent a traditional "nihon-ma" room and strut around in their Naruto costume, trying to convince Tokyoites that they're actually Japanese. No, this is, in fact, the worst sin you could ever commit against the Japanese people, the worst form of Weeaboo criminality that you could possibly perpetrate and is therefore a form of blasphemy that all true Otakus should revile and abhor.

To avoid committing such grievous and profane acts, you must study up on all the rich and myriad facets of Japanese society and cultivate a fertile knowledge of all things Japanese. This handbook is organized into chapters which, when taken together, provide all the information you'll ever need to develop that range of Japan-related knowledge and so forever save yourself from any possibility of suffering the Weeaboo fate. We'll begin that education with a complete delineation of one all-important topic of Japan-centered education: the rich tradition of Japanese cinema, theatre and entertainment arts.

3.2 The Early Days of Japanese Cinema

In the beginning, there were four. Film production in the 1940s and 50s was very director-based, in Japan. Directors would be paid, given a livelihood, and, in turn, would be expected to produce quality works for their studio. Even if their films flopped, they were still hired, still nurtured by their studio and still given license to express themselves, artistically. It was much different than the cut-throat, "it's all about money" culture of Hollywood and most of today's film industry. They wanted their films to enjoy popular success, of course, but really, it was about finding artists, giving them the best atmosphere to grow and letting the talent speak for itself. Usually, the level of talent this produced was sufficient to keep the public interested and the directors who grew up and evolved in this free and fertile atmosphere are still revered, today.

The four most revered directors of the period — at least in the west — were Akira Kurosawa, Kenji Mizoguchi, Yasojiro Ozu and Hiroshi Inagaki. Together, these pioneering directors brought Japanese cinema, the legend of the samurai and the first glimpses of modern Japanese culture to the west. Given their importance in encouraging true Japanophilia throughout the western world, it really is inexcusable for any true Otaku not to, at least, have a passing knowledge of them. To avoid such a gap in your knowledge, we'll now delve further into the biographies of these four directors, their styles and some of their most pivotal works.

Akira Kurosawa

Life: 1910 to 1988. Born in Tokyo.
Notable films: "Seven Samurai", "Yojimbo", "Rashomon".

Kurosawa is, by far, the most well-known Japanese director in the west — even up to the present day. His works are the most consumed, by western audiences. He was also the most influential director, as far as helping to transmit the Japanese culture to the west. His 30 epic films helped form the foundation of the modern Japanese film industry and he helped bring the legendary image of the samurai warrior to the west, through his many high-quality samurai epics.

Through such films as Seven Samurai, Yojimbo, Sanjuro, Ran and Kagemusha he practically defined the samurai (or chanbara) genre and these works inspired a great many Hollywood films, including The Dirty Dozen and a Fist Full of Dollars. Kurosawa came by his samurai legacy honestly, having been born into a traditional samurai family (one of the few still remaining in pre-war Japan). A large part of his mission was to not let the perspective of the samurai die, as it was passed down in his family, and so he arranged for it to live on, in these timeless examples of fine Japanese cinema.

Kurosawa knowledge is a requirement for any self-respecting Otaku. It is compulsory. Without an awareness of the significance of Kurosawa, as far as spreading Japanophilia goes, your knowledge is truly incomplete. That includes a familiarity with the films, the plot-lines and the main actors involved. No Otaku, for example, should be ignorant of who Toshiro Mifune is. If you are, then you are dangerously close to being a Weeaboo. Mifune is the iconic actor who came to symbolize the samurai warrior, in the eyes of the west, because Kurosawa had a tendency to use him as a leading man, in practically all of his samurai films. If you did not know that, then we recommend you educate yourself on all matters Mifune, without further ado, by looking up his films, and embarking on a Mifune marathon. We recommend Yojimbo, Sanjuro, Thrones of Blood, Seven Samurai and the Hidden Fortress as a great place to start. Watching these will educate you, quickly, not only on the subject of Toshiro Mifune, but on Akira Kurosawa, as well.

More than just the films, however, for the true Japanophile, getting to know Kurosawa's troupe of actors (the ones he regularly used in his films) is a real rite of passage. True regulars like Mifune, Takashi Shimura, Kyoko Kagawa, Kamatari Fujiwara, Tatsuya Nakadai, Isuzu Yamada and so many more. It becomes a genuine Japanophilic pleasure to be able to spot the actors, in older Japanese films, and mention them by name, with all the enthusiasm and minutiae of knowledge that accompanies true Otaku fandom.

Kenji Mizoguchi

Life: 1898 to 1956. Born in Tokyo.
Notable films: "Ugetsu", "Sansho the Bailiff", "The 47 Ronin".

Mizoguchi is perhaps the second most revered Japanese director, at least in the west. Much like Kurosawa, he did much to preserve the ethic and the sensibilities of traditional Japanese society, through such historical works as The 47 Ronin and Sansho the Bailiff, which were set in Japan's feudal past. The educated Otaku, familiar with Kurosawa's troupe of regular actors, will recognize some of these actors in Mizoguchi's films. Such as Kyoko Kagawa, in Sansho the

Bailiff and Daisuke Katō in The 47 Ronin. He even used Toshiro Mifune, in such films as Rickshaw Man and The Life of Oharu.

Mizoguchi was one of the first Japanese directors to win an award at the prestigious Venice Film Festival, for Ugetsu, in 1953. The first one was Kurosawa, who won at the Venice Film Festival in 1951, for Rashomon. This is why Kurosawa and Mizoguchi are considered the two directors most responsible for popularizing Japanese cinema, in the west. Otaku who wish to improve on their Japanophilia are recommended to learn about Mizoguchi by starting with Ugetsu. A ghost story, essentially, taking place in feudal Japan, it is steeped in the legends of ancient Japan, and should definitely enflame the soul of any true Japanophile, with its mystic imagery.

Yasojiro Ozu

Life: 1903 to 1963. Born in Tokyo.
Notable films: "Tokyo Story", "Early Spring", "Floating Weeds".

Of the big four, Ozu is the most subtle and is the best at capturing the subtle social drama of traditional Japanese society. His work, though focusing less on Japan's feudal past and on the chanbara themes popularized by Kurosawa and Mizoguchi, still gives an essential glimpse into the Japanese character. Many are fascinating period pieces, giving a rare peek into what the culture was like, from the late 20s, right up to the start of the 60s. Ozu focused more on the social graces and the intricacies of personal relationships. And so, any Japanophile who wants to witness the social foundation of Japan, almost in a first-hand way, can accomplish a lot by watching an epic Ozu work, such as Tokyo Story or Floating Weeds.

What is more, a lot of the same actors appear in his works, as did in Kurosawa and Mizoguchi's work. For example, Setsuko Hara, who starred in Kurosawa's film No Regrets for our Youth, was later made famous by Ozu, because he often used her as a leading lady, in what turned out to be his most popular works. Also, Kyoko Kagawa, who was later used by Kurosawa, on a regular basis, first

tasted fame for her role in Ozu's Tokyo Story. In fact, Tokyo Story is probably a great place to start. It is widely regarded as Ozu's masterpiece and is often cited as one of the greatest films ever made. It certainly is a fitting start, if you want a taste of that pre-western-exposure culture of Japan, which comes through so well in Ozu's films, maybe even more than with the other three directors.

Hiroshi Inagaki

Life: 1905 to 1980. Born in Tokyo.
Notable films: "Samurai Trilogy", "Birth of Japan", "Samurai Banners".

The last of the big four, Inagaki, although less prolific than the others, must hold a prominent place of honor, in any list of early Japanese directors. He holds the distinction of being the first early Japanese director to win an Academy Award, for his film Samurai I: Musashi Miyamoto, which starred none other than Toshiro Mifune, playing the legendary samurai, Musashi. This film, made in 1954, expanded into a trilogy, produced in color, which included other Kurosawa troupe actors, such as Daisuke Kato. Although Kurosawa was the king of chanbara/samurai epics, Inagaki popularized the highly dramatized, almost melodramatic samurai epic, which later became popular, in the west, and greatly influenced the later chanbara genre of manga and anime, as well as Hollywood films, like Kill Bill.

What is more, his film, The Birth of Japan, has been called Japan's answer to The Ten Commandments, in that it dramatizes the creation of Japan, based on the sacred texts and legends of the Shinto religion. As if this didn't qualify him as enough of a figure to revere, among Japanophiles, he also cast Toshiro Mifune as one of the prominent Shinto Gods in the film! Given all this, I don't think it's possible to be a full-blooded Japanophile, without first seeing Mifune play Musashi, in Inagaki's Samurai trilogy and without watching Mifune play a Shinto god in The Birth of Japan. And so, for that reason, we include him in our list of the top four early directors.

3.2.1 The Early Films

To help you in your Japanophile ambitions, we'll now list all the best early films, chronologically, from the "big four" directors.

The 47 Ronin

Director: Kenji Mizoguchi.
Year Created: 1941.
Produced by: Shochiku studio.
Genre: Chanbara/samurai, drama, action.
Starring: Chojuro Kawarasaki, Kanemon Nakamura, Ryu Okochi.
Description: This movie follows the famous events of the 47 retainers of Lord Asano, who was unjustly forced into ritual suicide, by another lord. The 47 samurai decided to get revenge, but chose to do it very carefully. Pretending to become dissolute alcoholics and various other kinds of fallen warriors, they actually plotted the assassination of their dead lord's enemy. After many years of this acting, the enemy lord was lulled into a sense of security and then they acted — avenging their dead lord's memory and restoring his honor. This tale is based on real historical fact, which is considered the "national tale" of Japan. It is such a perfect representation of samurai honor and nobility that it is cherished by the Japanese and has been told in countless movies, books and Kabuki dramas, since it first happened, in the 18th century.

Sanshiro Sugata

Director: Akira Kurosawa.
Year Created: 1943.
Produced by: Toho Studios.
Genre: Martial arts, action, drama.
Starring: Susumu Fujita, Denjiro Okochi, Takashi Shimura.
Description: The first film by the legendary director Akira Kurosawa. The hero, Sanshiro, is a brash young Judo student, who is powerful, but doesn't know how to use his strength. Under the tutelage of a wise, old Judo master, he learns that the meaning of life and the meaning of Judo are strangely entwined. This film is set in Meiji era Japan and is unique for its haunting atmosphere of discipline, traditional martial arts and old Japan.

Drunken Angel

Director: Akira Kurosawa.
Year Created: 1948.
Produced by: Toho Studios.
Genre: Drama, crime, tragedy.
Starring: Toshiro Mifune, Takashi Shimura, Noriko Sengoku.
Description: This is the first Kurosawa film to prominently feature Toshiro Mifune and is a great film for discovering what very young Mifune was like. In this tale, a reckless and violent gangster learns he has tuberculosis. As a result, he is forced into a bond with his doctor — who hates his gangster lifestyle, which is making his medical condition worse. The doctor tries his best to save the willful gangster's life.

Stray Dog

Director: Akira Kurosawa.
Year Created: 1949.
Produced by: Toho Studios.
Genre: Action, drama, crime, mystery.
Starring: Toshiro Mifune, Takashi Shimura, Ko Kimura.
Description: This is a kind of "film noir" detective movie by Akira Kurosawa. It is his first foray into detective fiction and one of our favorites. Once again, it features a very young Mifune, in all his glory. In this film, a young Tokyo detective is mortified to discover he has lost his service weapon. To make matters worse, it seems like his gun has fallen into the hands of a homicidal maniac, who is using it to kill innocent people. Racked with guilt, the detective enlists the help of an older detective to help him track down his gun and the murderer who has gotten hold of it.

Late Spring

Director: Yasujiro Ozu.
Year Created: 1949.
Produced by: Shôchiku Eiga studio.
Genre: Drama.
Starring: Chishu Ryu, Setsuko Hara, Haruko Sugimura.
Description: This early film of Yasujiro Ozu was based on a short story called "Father and Daughter" by Kasuo Hirotsu. It is of the "shōshimin-eiga" genre, a genre of Japanese film dealing with ordinary

The Japanophile's Handbook

people in the then modern era of post-war Japan. Ozu practically invented this genre and it typifies his films very well. This film is considered Ozu's most perfect example of this genre and one of his best films. This film tells the story of a 27 year old woman who lives with her widowed father. Although relatives and friends try a variety of tactics to convince her to marry, she is steadfast in her dutiful desire to care for her elderly father. This is also the first popular film where Ozu uses the actress Setsuko Hara. She later became his favorite leading lady.

Rashomon

Director: Akira Kurosawa.
Year Created: 1950.
Produced by: Daiei Film.
Genre: Action, drama, supernatural, chanbara/samurai.
Starring: Toshiro Mifune, Machiko Kyo, Masayuki Mori.
Description: This is one of Akira Kurosawa's most famous films. It won the Venice Film Festival award in 1951 and is one of the most acclaimed films of all time. Rashomon centers around a rape, committed by a bandit, against a samurai's wife. The story takes the form of the three people involved appearing before a judge, explaining their side of the story. As each person's story is so different, it becomes a real puzzle who is telling the truth — who is really the guilty party and who the real victim is.

The Men Who Tread on the Tiger's Tail

Director: Akira Kurosawa.
Year Created: 1952.
Produced by: Toho Studios.
Genre: Drama, action, chanbara/samurai.
Starring: Takashi Shimura, Susumu Fujita, Denjiro Okochi.
Description: This is based on an old Kabuki theater play. In this story, a member of the Japanese royal family is trying to escape an enemy. As a way of accomplishing this, his generals dress up like a party of monks and escort him through the woods. But, when encountering the enemy, the generals must resort to the unthinkable, in order to save their lord's life.

The Life of Oharu

<u>Director:</u> Kenji Mizoguchi.
<u>Year Created:</u> 1952.
<u>Produced by:</u> Shintoho studio.
<u>Genre:</u> Drama, action, chanbara/samurai.
<u>Starring:</u> Kinuyo Tanaka, Toshiro Mifune, Takashi Shimura.
<u>Description:</u> This film by Kenji Mizoguchi was based on a novel by
Ihara Saikaku. It tells the tale of a woman named Oharu, who was
formerly a concubine for a feudal lord. We follow her struggles as she
tries to escape the shame brought by her life in prostitution, which her
father had forced her into.

Tokyo Story

<u>Director:</u> Yasujiro Ozu.
<u>Year Created:</u> 1953.
<u>Produced by:</u> Shokiku studio.
<u>Genre:</u> Drama.
<u>Starring:</u> Setsuko Hara, Kyoko Kagawa, Cheiko Higashiyama.
<u>Description:</u> This is another of Ozu's masterpieces and is considered,
by some to be one the greatest films ever made. Once again using
Setsuko Hara as a leading lady, it also featured a very young Kyoko
Kagawa — later to be used by Kurosawa in many films. In this tale, an
elderly couple from the country visit their adult children in Tokyo. The
busy children are dismissive of the parents, however, and try to fob
them off on each other. Only their widowed daughter-in-law, played by
Hara, treats them kindly.

Ugetsu

<u>Director:</u> Kenji Mizoguchi.
<u>Year Created:</u> 1953.
<u>Produced by:</u> Daiei Film.
<u>Genre:</u> Drama, supernatural, action, chanbara/samurai.
<u>Starring:</u> Masayuki Mori, Machiko Kyo, Kinuyo Tanaka.
<u>Description:</u> This peerless classic by Kenji Mizoguchi is arguably his
greatest work. It is a tale of war, love and the supernatural. Following
two couples, in feudal Japan, it shows what destruction can be brought
to our families, when we let money, power and ambition inspire our
actions. This is a great film for Japanophiles, as it involves samurai, old

Japan and supernatural creatures from out of Shinto and Buddhist mythology.

Seven Samurai

Director: Akira Kurosawa.
Year Created: 1954.
Produced by: Toho Studios.
Genre: Action, adventure, drama, chanbara/samurai.
Starring: Toshiro Mifune, Takashi Shimura, Daisuke Kato.
Description: This is undoubtedly Akira Kurosawa's most famous film. It defined the Chanbara genre of film and has influenced countless directors, after him. In fact, even the Hollywood Western "The Magnificent Seven" was based on this movie. It is absolutely essential that all Japanophiles watch this film at least once. The plot goes, a poor village of farmers are at the mercy of a ruthless band of brigands. The village elder tells the farmers to go to the city and hire samurai warriors to help defend the city. Eventually, seven very unique characters are gathered together and they set to work defeating the brigands, once and for all.

Sansho the Bailiff

Director: Kenji Mizoguchi.
Year Created: 1954.
Produced by: Daiei Film.
Genre: Chanbara/Samurai, drama, action.
Starring: Kinuyo Tanaka, Yoshikata Yoda, Kyoko Kagawa.
Description: Another great film by Mizoguchi, this one is about two children who are sold into slavery, when their governor father is forced into exile. The two children grow up in the slave camp and develop very different philosophies on life, eventually trying to find their mother, who was rumored to have been forced into prostitution, when their father was first exiled.

Samurai Trilogy

Director: Hiroshi Inagaki
Year Created: 1954.
Produced by: Toho Studios.
Genre: Chanbara/Samurai, Drama, Romance, Action.
Starring: Toshiro Mifune, Rentaro Mikuni, Kōji Tsuruta.

Description: Composed of three films: Samurai I: Musashi Miyamoto (1954), Samurai II: Duel at Ichijoji Temple (1955) and Samurai III: Duel at Ganryu Island (1956). These films later influenced such Hollywood films as Kill Bill. In it, we follow the career and growth of the famous samurai master Musashi Miyamoto (played by Toshiro Mifune). From his humble beginnings, as a simple strong-arm, Musashi develops into a self-disciplined and polished warriors, in the best traditions of the noble Bushido warrior. The first film in this series won the 1955 Academy Award for best foreign language film and the trilogy is based on a novel by Eiji Yoshikawa.

Early Spring

Director: Yasujiro Ozu.
Year Created: 1956.
Produced by: Shokiku studio.
Genre: Drama.
Starring: Chikage Awajima, Ryo Ikebe, Keiko Kishi.
Description: This film by Ozu was the first film to deal significantly with the hardships of the famously workaholic Japanese "salaryman." In it, a young salaryman and his wife struggle to keep their marriage alive, in the midst of his demanding profession. At the same time, he is tempted to pursue a mistress, on the side, in order to help him deal with the many stresses of his professional life.

Thrones of Blood

Director: Akira Kurosawa.
Year Created: 1957.
Produced by: Toho Studios.
Genre: Action, adventure, supernatural, chanbara/samurai.
Starring: Toshiro Mifune, Isuzu Yamada, Takashi Shimura.
Description: Kurosawa was a fan of Shakespeare and often wrote films, set in feudal Japan, but based on Shakespeare plays. This story was based on Macbeth and tells the story of a samurai general, whose ambitious wife leads him to commit treason against his own lord. Following the prophecy of an evil witch, the general becomes lord of Spider's Web Castle, but is perplexed by the meaning of the witch's final prophecy, which stipulates the only condition in which the general's reign might come to an end. This movie is a truly fantastic example of both Kurosawa's and Mifune's prowess and is highly

recommended for all Otaku to watch at least once.

Rickshaw Man

Director: Hiroshi Inagaki
Year Created: 1958.
Produced by: Toho Studios.
Genre: Drama, romance.
Starring: Toshiro Mifune, Hideko Takamine.
Description: In this Inagaki film, a poor rickshaw driver (played by Mifune) helps a rich family go back and forth between doctor appointments. But, when the father dies, the rickshaw man finds he has to take on the responsibilities of the father, in order to keep the family he has come to love together.

The Hidden Fortress

Director: Akira Kurosawa.
Year Created: 1958.
Produced by: Toho Studios.
Genre: Action, adventure, chanbara/samurai.
Starring: Toshiro Mifune, Misa Uehara, Kamatari Fugiwara.
Description: Another iconic Kurosawa film, this one follows the zany adventures of two greedy peasants, as they search for gold. Based in feudal Japan, these two hapless buffoons soon find themselves caught up in an epic struggle between a local royal princess and her enemies. The princess' general, trying to lead his princess to safety, enlists the help of the peasants, in transporting her away from the authorities that are endeavoring to capture her. This film is widely believed to have served as a partial inspiration to George Lucas, in the creation of his first Star Wars film. And, if you watch both films, you can definitely see some of the common elements there.

Floating Weeds

Director: Yasujiro Ozu.
Year Created: 1959.
Produced by: Daiei Film.
Genre: Drama.
Starring: Ganjiro Nakamura, Machiko Kyo, Ayako Wakao.
Description: In this film, the head of a Kabuki acting troupe arrives on

The Japanophile's Handbook

an island in modern Japan, to publicize their latest performance. Meeting up with an old mistress, he realizes that he fathered a son with her, years ago. The son now works in the post office and the actor is struck with a strong desire to make up for lost time, and take on the role of his father. The actor's current mistress, however, who is also the lead actress of his Kabuki troupe becomes viciously jealous and tries her best to sabotage the situation.

The Birth of Japan

Director: Hiroshi Inagaki
Year Created: 1959.
Produced by: Toho Studios.
Genre: Fantasy epic, Shinto spiritualism.
Starring: Toshiro Mifune, Yoko Tsukasa, Akihiko Hirata.
Description: This film is based on Shinto mythology, telling the cosmological tale of how Japan came into existence. Given this is the actual Shinto version of Japan's creation, this is an Otaku must-see. Couple that with the fact that one of the Shinto gods, Susanoo, is played by Japanese acting god Toshiro Mifune, and you basically can't possibly miss out on this one! It has been called Japan's answer to the Old Testament Bible film "The Ten Commandments." Given the complex mythology, this film is complicated, but culminates in a harrowing scene where Susanoo needs to fight a legendary eight-headed dragon, one of the most ferocious and fearsome creatures in all of Shinto mythology.

Yojimbo

Director: Akira Kurosawa.
Year Created: 1961.
Produced by: Toho Studios.
Genre: Action, adventure, drama, chanbara/samurai.
Starring: Toshiro Mifune, Tatsuya Nakadai, Isuzu Yamada.
Description: This is another one of those Kurosawa films which all self-respecting Otaku should see, at least once, in order to be full-fledged members of the Japanophile club. It is one of his most iconic works and probably Mifune's finest performance. In this film, a clever ronin uses guts and strategy to empty a town of warring gangsters. By getting them to fight each other, and killing off the rest, he single-handedly cleanses the town of the gangster's noxious influence. This classic

inspired the Hollywood film "A Fistful of Dollars." Its sequel, "Sanjuro", was produced one year later.

The Story of Osaka Castle

Director: Hiroshi Inagaki
Year Created: 1961.
Produced by: Toho Studios.
Genre: Chanbara/Samurai, Drama, Romance, Action.
Starring: Toshiro Mifune, Kyoko Kagawa, Akihiko Hirata.
Description: This film is based on historical fact and is set in Japan in the 1600s. The hero, played by Mifune, is an independent-minded ronin, who wanders into Osaka, searching for a new life. He winds up walking into a covert plan, designed by the Toyotomi clan, who are seeking to stop the insane territorial ambitions of the famous Lord Ieyasu Tokugawa.

Sanjuro

Director: Akira Kurosawa.
Year Created: 1962.
Produced by: Toho Studios.
Genre: Action, adventure, drama, chanbara/samurai.
Starring: Toshiro Mifune, Tatsuya Nakadai, Takashi Shimura.
Description: The sequel to Yojimbo, this film is almost like a more elaborate replay of Yojimbo, because it uses most of the same actors of the first film, but in all different roles (except for the protagonist, Mifune, who is the same swaggering ronin character). In this installment, the ronin is joined by a group of nine young samurai, who are all friends and all part of the same clan. The ronin helps them to free their framed uncle and outwit the corrupt chamberlain who framed him. In doing so, the ronin ruins the chamberlain and must then duel with his powerful general, out for revenge.

An Autumn Afternoon

Director: Yasujiro Ozu.
Year Created: 1962.
Produced by: Shochiku studio.
Genre: Drama.
Starring: Shima Iwashita, Chishu Ryu, Keiji Sada.
Description: In this Ozu film, he once again explores the older

father/spinster daughter dynamic, but takes it in another direction. In this story, a young woman takes care of her elderly father, but he is very aware of the fact that he is obligated to find her a good husband. He begins to feel he is being selfish by holding on to her and taking advantage of her sense of duty to her father — so denying her the joys of having her own family. The patriarch then tries his best to make up for lost time and find her a husband.

High and Low

Director: Akira Kurosawa.
Year Created: 1963.
Produced by: Toho Studios.
Genre: Drama, Crime, Mystery.
Starring: Toshiro Mifune, Kyoko Kagawa, Tatsuya Nakadai.
Description: This is another fine example of Kurosawa's grasp of the Detective and Crime genre. Featuring many troupe regulars, like Mifune, Tatsya Nakadai, Kyoko Kagawa (and even Susumu Fujita, who played Sanshiro Sugata), this film is a real treat for Kurosawa fans! It is loosely based on the novel "King's Ransom" by Ed Bain. In this film, a wealthy shoe executive named Gondo (played by Mifune) is poised to win a major coup, by buying out the company he works for, when he is suddenly extorted by a kidnapper, who claims to have kidnapped his son. It's soon revealed the kidnapper made a mistake and took his chauffeur's son, instead. The cruel kidnapper still demands payment, however, or he will kill the child. Gondo must decide if he's willing to throw away his fortune in order to save his chauffeur's son and Tokyo detectives (headed by Nakadai) do their best to track down the criminal.

The End of Summer

Director: Yasujiro Ozu.
Year Created: 1961.
Produced by: Toho Studios.
Genre: Drama.
Starring: Setsuko Hara, Ganjiro Nakamura, Yoko Tsukasa.
Description: This film by Ozu is considered a masterly combination of comedy and tragedy. An older man, who runs a brewery, is somewhat childlike in his demeanor. His many children often worry about his life choices and are particularly upset when they discover that he has gotten into the habit of visiting an old mistress, from his youth. They interfere,

hoping to protect him from his own folly, but their actions backfire.

Red Beard

Director: Akira Kurosawa.
Year Created: 1965.
Produced by: Toho Studios.
Genre: Drama.
Starring: Toshiro Mifune, Kyoko Kagawa, Yuzo Kayama.
Description: This was the last Kurosawa film to feature Toshiro Mifune as the leading man. After this film, it has been reported that Mifune and Kurosawa fell out and so Mifune ended his long career as Kurosawa's favorite leading man. This tale, set in 19th century Japan, takes place in a medical clinic. A young, ambitious doctor is annoyed to work in a poor clinic, but is soon brought around to understand the true meaning of medical service, under the wise tutelage of Red Beard, the gruff head doctor, played by Mifune. This touching film is one of our favorites.

Samurai Banners

Director: Hiroshi Inagaki.
Year Created: 1969.
Produced by: Toho Studios.
Genre: Chanbara/samurai, drama, action.
Starring: Toshiro Mifune, Yorozuya Kinnosuke.
Description: This film is based on the life of the 15th century military general, Yamamoto Kansuke. Played by Toshiro Mifune, the general is a ruthless warrior, who is brilliant at strategy. He advises lord Takeda Shingen on practically everything, from battle plans to who should be assassinated. Eventually a love triangle develops between the lord, the general and a princess who was once doomed to ritual suicide, but refused to submit.

Kagemusha

Director: Akira Kurosawa.
Year Created: 1980.
Produced by: Toho Studios.
Genre: Action, chanbara/samurai, political drama.
Starring: Tatsuya Nakadai, Tsutomo Yamazaki, Daisuke Ryu.
Description: In this later film by Kurosawa, long-time Kurosawa troupe

actor Tatsuya Nakadai has come to replace Toshiro Mifune as his new leading man. He will also play the lead in Kurosawa's "Ran", five years later. In this film, a petty thief gets caught up in national politics when he is discovered to be an exact double for the ruling lord. The lord, amused by their similarity, brings the thief to live in his royal court. Unfortunately, the lord soon dies. Needing to maintain the illusion that the lord is alive, for political reasons, the humble thief is forced to assume the disguise of the deceased lord. Reluctantly, the thief assumes the great responsibility and discovers how hard it is to live a lord's life.

Ran

Director: Akira Kurosawa.
Year Created: 1985.
Produced by: Toho Studios.
Genre: Drama, action, chanbara/samurai.
Starring: Tatsuya Nakadai, Akira Terao, Daisuke Ryu.
Description: This film by Akira Kurosawa continues his custom of translating Shakespeare into feudal Japanese history. This story is based on King Lear, but follows the tale of an elderly Japanese Lord, who abdicates his throne — dividing it among his three sons. Sadly, his sons refuse to share and share alike, as his father has instructed them. Instead, two sons turn against the old lord and his life ends in the same tragic way as King Lear's.

3.3 Modern Japanese Cinema

Nowadays, there are so many notable directors that it is hard to summarize them into a "top four", the way we did with the early directors. But, given this is a book for western Japanophiles, we will just list the four most popular directors, who have found a large audience, in the west. In our view, the four most influential Japanese directors, of the modern age, are Takeshi Kitano, Kinji Fukasaku, Hirokazu Koreeda and Takashi Miike. To further help our Otaku brethren, to further expand their knowledge, we will now list the best films from among these modern directors. Listed chronologically, we recommend all prospective Otakus watch these films or at least make an effort to learn about the directors.

Swords of Vengeance (*Akō-jō danzetsu*)

Director: Kinji Fukasaku.
Year Created: 1978.
Produced by: Toei Company.
Genre: Action, chanbara/samurai, drama.
Starring: Kinnosuke Yorozuya, Sonny Chiba, Toshiro Mifune.
Description: This is a more modern re-telling of the historical tale of
the 47 Ronin. It is, basically, a remake of Kenji Mizoguchi's film, "The
47 Ronin." It is even more notable, however, for featuring the one and
only Toshiro Mifune, in one of his later film roles. As in the other film,
it tells the story of the loyal 47 samurai warriors, who avenged Lord
Asano, when he was unjustly forced to commit ritual suicide. Based on
historical fact and the many traditional Japanese plays, based on the
same story.

Shogun's Samurai

Director: Kinji Fukasaku.
Year Created: 1978.
Produced by: Toei Company.
Genre: Action, chanbara/samurai, drama.
Starring: Toshiro Mifune, Sonny Chiba, Kinnosuke Yorozuya.
Description: This is another great historical film, distinctive for
featuring both the legend of old Japanese cinema, Toshiro Mifune, and
the famous star of modern Japanese cinema, Sonny Chiba, together in
one film. It is based on the rivalry between two nobles of the Tokugawa
period. The two brothers, hoping to succeed to the status of Shogun,
use strategy and dirty tactics to try to undercut the other. The Yagyu
clan, which provide the family with most of their muscle, wind up
becoming an important pawn in this battle between noble brothers.

Samurai Reincarnation

Director: Kinji Fukasaku.
Year Created: 1981.
Produced by: Toei Company.
Genre: Action, chanbara/samurai, drama, supernatural.
Starring: Sonny Chiba, Kenji Sawada.
Description: The first major samurai film to go into zombie territory,
although they aren't exactly zombies. This film stars Sonny Chiba and is

set in the Tokugawa period. After the historical Shimabara rebellion, where many Christians were slaughtered, a samurai survivor, named Shito, renounces God, for turning his back on them and allowing them to be slaughtered. The samurai makes a pact with Satan, asking for vengeance. This dark pact gives him the power to raise the dead, in order to help him get his revenge. After much carnage, the son of Shito tries to discover a way to deal with the vast armies of undead, which his father unleashed upon the world.

Legend of the Eight Samurai

<u>Director:</u> Kinji Fukasaku.
<u>Year Created:</u> 1983.
<u>Produced by:</u> Toei Company.
<u>Genre:</u> Fantasy, action, martial arts, historical.
<u>Starring:</u> Hiroko Yakushimaru, Hiroyuki Sanada, Sonny Chiba.
<u>Description:</u> Continuing his theme of undead in ancient Japan, this story is about Princess Shizu, whose whole family has fallen victim to an army of vengeful undead. An ancient artifact points her in the direction of eight samurai who can help her deal with the evil queen who is in charge of these undead hoards. This evil queen lives in a castle guarded by all kinds of supernatural creatures, but with the eight chosen samurai, they venture forth on their quest to defeat this dark queen.

Violent Cop

<u>Director:</u> Takeshi Kitano.
<u>Year Created:</u> 1989.
<u>Produced by:</u> Shochiku Studios.
<u>Genre:</u> Crime, drama, action.
<u>Starring:</u> Takeshi Kitano, Maiko Kawakami, Makoto Ashikawa.
<u>Description:</u> This is the break-out film of Takeshi Kitano, who later became famous for his gritty, violent crime dramas, usually featuring police and yakuza (Japanese gangsters). In this first film, an unconventional police officer (played by Kitano, himself) has a tendency to break the rules, often resorting to excessive violence to clean up the city. Unfortunately, he soon discovers that his own partner is in business with the underworld.

 # The Japanophile's Handbook

Sonatine

Director: Takeshi Kitano.
Year Created: 1993.
Produced by: Shochiku Studios.
Genre: Crime, drama, action.
Starring: Takeshi Kitano, Aya Kokumai, Tetsu Watanabe.
Description: This gritty Yakuza film by Takeshi Kitano is the violent story of a group of gangsters sent to Okinawa to mediate a dispute. However, the enforcer (played by Kitano) doesn't believe he's been sent there for that reason. He suspects he is being set up to be removed from the gang, by force. As conflict escalates, the conflicting personalities of the gang take refuge in a beach house, where a tense standoff of nerves plays out, as no one is entirely sure what the secret plan is, or who is going to be taken out.

Maborosi

Director: Hirokazu Koreeda.
Year Created: 1995.
Produced by: Milestone Films.
Genre: Drama.
Starring: Makiko Esumi, Tadanobu Asano, Akira Emoto.
Description: This film, by Hirokazu Koreeda, won a best director award at the 1995 Venice Film Festival. A young woman's husband dies, by getting hit by a train. She can never be sure if he committed suicide. After her second marriage, she is tortured by this question, not understanding why he would do it, when his life was not unhappy. Looking for meaning, she embarks on a dark journey of reflection, alongside her new husband.

Hana-bi (Fireworks)

Director: Takeshi Kitano.
Year Created: 1997.
Produced by: Nippon Herald Films.
Genre: Crime, drama, action.
Starring: Takeshi Kitano, Kayoko Kishimoto, Ren Osugi.
Description: Another film directed by Takeshi Kitano, he reprises his role as a violent police detective. The cop, Nishi, suffers a terrible setback in his career and retires prematurely. In his retirement, he has to

take care of his terminally ill wife, as well as dealing with the Yakuza, who he has relied upon to give him the money he needs to keep his wife alive.

After Life

Director: Hirokazu Koreeda.
Year Created: 1998.
Produced by: Engine Films.
Genre: Fantasy, drama.
Starring: Erika Oda, Susumu Terajima, Takashi Naito.
Description: This imaginative film, by Hirokazu Koreeda, takes place in the afterlife. In this story, people who die are obliged to spend a week with an afterlife counselor, in order to review their lives and carefully select one single memory, which they are then allowed to retain, into eternity.

Battle Royale

Director: Kinji Fukasaku.
Year Created: 2000.
Produced by: Toei Company.
Genre: Action, thriller..
Starring: Takeshi Kitano, Tatsuya Fujiwara, Aki Maeda.
Description: This film is very famous, in Japan, and is considered an iconic work. Although directed by Kinji Fukasaku, it features Takeshi Kitano, as an actor. In this story, the Japanese government of the future forces high school students to battle each other. This film was banned in several countries, when it first came out, but was a blockbuster hit in Japan.

Zatoichi

Director: Takeshi Kitano.
Year Created: 2003.
Produced by: Shochiku studio.
Genre: Crime, drama, action.
Starring: Takeshi Kitano, Tadanobu Asano, Yui Natsukawa.
Description: Another Kitano film, this film follows the life of Zatoichi, a blind swordsman. This swordsman comes to the rescue of a town in the grip of a group of yakuza. Delving into the history of the town, he

soon determines that all the yakuza need to be wiped out, in punishment for their many crimes.

Zebraman

Director: Takashi Miike.
Year Created: 2004.
Produced by: Toei Company.
Genre: Fantasy, drama, action.
Starring: Sho Aikawa, Kyoka Suzuki, Atsuro Watanabe.
Description: In this film, a failed 3rd grade teacher has his life changed when he discovers that it is his destiny to become the real-life Zebraman — an old TV superhero. Using his newfound powers, he is the only one that can rescue the planet from an alien invasion.

Izo

Director: Takashi Miike.
Year Created: 2004.
Produced by: Izo Partners.
Genre: Fantasy, drama, action, samurai.
Starring: Kazuya Nakayama, Takeshi Kitano, Kaori Momoi.
Description: This film by Takashi Miike also features Kitano, as an actor. This film is based on a historical figure, Izo Okada, who lived in the 1800s and was tortured and killed, for being an assassin. This film follows the surreal, afterlife adventures of the tormented warrior. In a way, it is a throwback to the "warrior" plays of Noh theater, where a dead warrior petitions a priest to pray for him. Izo is a surreal and fascinating film.

The Great Yokai War

Director: Takashi Miike.
Year Created: 2005.
Produced by: Shochiku/Kadokawa Pictures.
Genre: Fantasy, adventure.
Starring: Junichi Okada, Rie Miyazawa.
Description: This film by Takashi Miike is a great film for all Otaku interested in Shinto and Japanese mythology! The Yokai are supernatural spirits. And, in this film, a young boy teams up with Yokai spirits, in order to fulfill his destiny as a great crusader for good.

Tapping into the power of the mythical Yokai of lore, the boy forges ahead on his quest to abolish evil spirits from the Earth.

Hana (The Tale of a Reluctant Samurai)

Director: Hirokazu Koreeda.
Year Created: 2006.
Produced by: Shochiku studio.
Genre: Action, martial art, samurai, drama.
Starring: Junichi Okada, Rie Miyazawa.
Description: This is a different samurai film, in that the protagonist must decide if he wants to use violence, or forgive the people who have wronged him. Soza, the hero, is sent on a mission of revenge, to avenge his father. Although Soza is not a strong swordsman, he embarks on the mission anyways. But when he does meet the man who killed his father, he has to decide if he wants to walk the path of peace or the path of blood.

Still Walking

Director: Hirokazu Koreeda.
Year Created: 2008.
Produced by: IFC Films.
Genre: Drama.
Starring: Hiroshi Abe, Yui Natsukawa.
Description: This film is a family drama. After many years apart, a group of siblings have come to visit their elderly parents, along with their young families. They meet to commemorate the death, by drowning, of their long lost brother, years ago. But they find they have all changed, subtly.

Air Doll

Director: Hirokazu Koreeda.
Year Created: 2009.
Produced by: Asmik Ace Entertainment.
Genre: Fantasy, drama.
Starring: Takeshi Kitano, Kippei Shiina, Tomokazu Miura.
Description: This film has some extra Otaku appeal, because it is based on a manga comic, called Kuuki Ningy by Yoshiie Goda, which was

serialized in the seinen manga magazine, Big Comic Original. In this film, an inflatable sex doll comes to life and leaves the home of the man who bought her and inadvertently brought her to life. She then mingles with regular people and gets a job at a video store, eventually falling in love with one of her co-workers.

13 Assassins

Director: Takashi Miike.
Year Created: 2010.
Produced by: Toho studio.
Genre: Action, drama, chanbara/samurai.
Starring: Koji Yakusho, Takayuki Yamada, Yusuke Iseya.
Description: This is a historical film, set in Tokugawa Japan, in the 1800s. In it, a samurai, who is disgusted by a corrupt young lord and his tendency to use his position to commit unthinkable crimes, assembles a group of assassins to execute some vigilante justice upon the untouchable lord.

Outrage

Director: Takeshi Kitano.
Year Created: 2010.
Produced by: Office Kitano/Warner Bros.
Genre: Crime, drama, action.
Starring: Takeshi Kitano, Kippei Shiina, Tomokazu Miura.
Description: In this Kitano film, yakuza bosses battle for power, by sucking up to the most powerful gangster family. Scheming and making allegiances, they all try to outdo each other and rise to the top of the criminal underworld. This is a film about the elaborate webs of loyalties, betrayals and cut-throat competition, which defines the Japanese underworld.

Yakuza Apocalypse

Director: Takashi Miike.
Year Created: 2015.
Produced by: Toho studio.
Genre: Action, crime, drama, supernatural.
Starring: Koji Yakusho, Takayuki Yamada, Yusuke Iseya.
Description: Kitano's first foray into the supernatural, this is a Kitano

yakuza film with a twist! In this film, the biggest yakuza boss there is, boss Kamiura, is known for being unusual. He is never seen outdoors and is known to have a mysterious skin disease. But in reality, he is a blood-sucking vampire. However, a lot of the gang don't know his secret and look down on him for what they mistakenly perceive to be health problems. A competing syndicate sends an anime-Otaku yakuza assassin to kill Kamiura, using their knowledge of his vampire condition. This assassin succeeds in killing him, but gets infected by the vampire and soon becomes one himself. Learning of his inheritance of vampirism, he decides to avenge his vampire predecessor and begins a campaign of vengeance against his former bosses.

3.4 Traditional Japanese Theater

In addition to cinema, Japan has a powerful tradition of theater, and its primary forms of traditional theater — Kabuki and Noh — still exert a powerful influence on the culture. You will often see elements and features of traditional Kabuki, popping up in manga, anime, Japanese films and video games. And so, if you want to be a truly in-the-know Otaku, who can spot these cultural references wherever they may turn up, you need to know at least a bit about these rich traditions of the Japanese theatrical arts.

3.4.1 Kabuki Theater

Beginning in 1603 AD, Kabuki originally involved only women, and was a bawdy, ribald form of entertainment art. Similar to burlesque shows that were popular in the west in the early 20th century, the Kabuki shows were places for people to meet in order to see risqué performances. Although they certainly had that element, and were often performed by prostitutes, they were also legitimate art forms. The word Ka-bu-ki stands for Sing, Dance and Skill, and this demonstrates the actual talents involved in Kabuki performance. It was much more than just the occasional bawdy joke and soon evolved into a truly respectable and sophisticated form of theater.

After being banned by the Shogunate because of its close links to the geisha girls, and prostitution, Kabuki continued to evolve into a new form. It became an all-male form of theater, due to the government ban on women performing it. During this time, a lot of the bawdy content was removed and it slowly metamorphosized into an even more elaborate art, requiring even greater skills.

By the time the ban on women performing Kabuki was revoked, Kabuki had already established itself as a national art form. Once again able to feature both male and female actors, Kabuki then entered a golden age, which lasted from 1673 to the late 1800s. Kabuki theater, although experiencing ups and downs, since then, has never died out, in Japan, and continues to be performed today.

Most of the grotesque masks (the white faced, colorfully-adorned Japanese characters) which we've seen in so many movies, anime and video games have their origin in Kabuki imagery. The truly dedicated Otaku, although not required to do so, would go far in cementing their deep Japanophilia, to truly soul-deep levels, by actually watching Kabuki performed. Such research will really give you an above average understanding both of the Japanese national temperament and an endless slew of cultural references in pop culture. The three most famous plays are Kanadehon Chushingura, Yoshitsune Senbon Zakura and Sugawara Denju Tenarai Kagami.

Kanadehon Chushingura (Treasury of Loyal Retainers) is the famous story of the 47 Ronin, which was immortalized in the two versions of the film, outlined above. The original story was remembered, thanks to Kabuki. The ronin, led by Oishi Kuranosuke, track down their enemy and exact revenge upon him before committing seppuku as required by their code of honor upon the death of their lord, Lord Takuminokami of the Asano clan.

Yoshitsune Senbon Zakura (Yoshitsune and the Thousand Cherry Trees) follows Minamoto no Yoshitsune as he flees from agents of his brother Yoritomo. Three Taira clan generals supposedly killed in the Genpei War, figure prominently, as their deaths ensure a complete end to the war and the arrival of peace, as does a Kitsune fox, named Genkurō.

Sugawara Denju Tenarai Kagami (Sugawara and the Secrets of Calligraphy) is based on the life of famed scholar Sugawara no Michizane (845–903), who is exiled from Kyoto, and upon his death causes a number of calamities in the capital. He is then deified, as Tenjin, kami (divine spirit) of scholarship, and worshipped in order to propitiate his angry spirit.

3.4.2 Noh Theater

Noh means "skill", "craft" or "talent" and that indicates what Noh theater is all about. It is, truly, the original Japanese theater and has been around since the 8th century AD. It's an esthetic and an art form that has been in continuous development for 13 centuries. Like Kabuki, Noh also involves masks and traditional Japanese costumes. However, unlike Kabuki, which is feudal Japan's answer to vaudeville, with its melodrama and its sensationalistic features, Noh has served as a genuine conduit for Japanese folklore and the religion of Shinto, for countless generations. Much of Noh are depictions of supernatural tales, featuring gods, demons and ghosts, which have been around, since long before the 8th century. There is another type of play, called Kyogen, which is derived from Noh, but more likely to involve comedy. For simplicity's sake, we'll stick to the original Noh theater, since it is the art form which Kyogen originated from. But it's recommended you learn about Kyogen too.

If you want to go that extra mile, into true understanding of Shinto, the national and indigenous religion of Japan, then you absolutely need to acquaint yourself with Noh theater. Here is where all the oldest, strangest and most magical tales of Japan's history are to be found. Kabuki may be a great way of understanding Japan's social world and its temperament, but Noh defines its soul, its heart and its deepest origins. Noh is a complex and elaborate art and so it will not be fully explained within the limited scope of this handbook, but all Otaku are encouraged to study Noh theater.

In the interest of helping you achieve that noble end, we'll outline the main types of Noh plays, here, as well as some of the most famous and popular plays, so you can seek them out, on your own.

3.4.2.1 Types of Noh Plays

Kami Mono (god plays) or waki Noh typically feature the actor in the role of a deity to tell the mythic story of a shrine or praise a particular god. Many of them structured in two acts, the deity takes a human form in disguise in the first act and reveals the real self in the second act. (e.g. Takasago, Chikubushima).

Shura mono (warrior plays) or ashura Noh takes its name from the Buddhist underworld. The protagonist appearing as a ghost of a famous samurai pleads to a monk for salvation and the drama culminates in a glorious re-enactment of the scene of his death in a full war costume. (e.g. Tamura, Atsumori).

Katsura mono (wig plays) or onna mono (woman plays) depict the actor in a female role and feature some of the most refined songs and dances in all of Noh, reflecting the smooth and flowing movements representing female characters. (e.g. Basho, Matsukaze)·

Kiri Noh (final plays) or oni mono (demon plays) usually feature the main actor in the role of monsters, goblins, or demons, and are often selected for their bright colors and fast-paced, tense finale movements. Kiri Noh is performed the last in a five-play program. There are roughly 30 plays in this category, most of which are shorter than the plays in the other categories.

3.4.2.2 Famous Noh Plays

Aoi no Ue (Lady Aoi). This is based on the famous Japanese novel, "The Tale of Genji." It is about Lady Rukujo, who is a mistress of the married Prince Genji. When his wife, Lady Aio, humiliates her and enrages her by telling her she is pregnant, the wildly jealous Lady Rukujo leaves her body and possesses Lady Aio, resulting in Lady Aio's death.

Aya no Tsuzumi (The Damask Drum). This is a supernatural tale about a humble gardener, who works at the palace of Chukuzen. During the course of his duties, he meets an royal concubine and promptly falls in love with her. Finding his infatuation amusing, the concubine toys with his affections. She sends him a message saying she

will hide a drum somewhere on the grounds and he can meet with her in a rendezvous if he just plays the drum. Finding it is some kind of drum that makes no sound, the gardener is humiliated and enraged. He drowns himself in torment and comes back to haunt the concubine.

Dojoji (Dojo Temple). This is a supernatural tale about an evil female spirit. This spirit causes all kinds of hauntings at a Buddhist temple, causing bells to fall and other commotion. This spirit is hoping to force a monk she has become infatuated with to reciprocate her love. Using the powers of his faith, the monk tries his best to resist the aggression of this amorous demon.

Hagoromo (The Feathered Mantle). In this supernatural tale, a fisherman finds a magic feather, dropped from the mythical "tennin" which is a kind of sky spirit. The tennin, however, has seen the fisherman take the feather and demands it back. Because the tennin cannot return to where it came from without the feather, the fisherman realizes he has an advantage and demands, in return, to learn the fabled dance of the tennins.

Izutsu (The Well Cradle). This tale centers around a priest, visiting the temples of Nara. in his journeys, he meets an old woman at a grave. She tells him a tale from hundreds of years ago. Then she admits that she is one of the characters from this ancient story, who died centuries ago. She then vanishes. The priest, shocked, asks the locals about it. They suggest he pray for her soul and so attract her to him, again. He does so and the woman appears, performing a dance and song about how her love for her husband has kept her spirit alive, always tending his grave.

Shōjō (The Tippling Demon). This is an interesting tale about a supernatural demon called a shōjō, which resembles an orangutan. In this story, the demon gets drunk and start dancing, wildly. He rewards the sake dealer who gave him the drink, by giving him unusual wooden dolls. These dolls (nara ningyō), are actually common charms, in Japan, and are used to ward off all kind of evils.

Takasago (Twin Pines). In this tale, a priest visits a shrine, at Takasago. There, he finds an elderly couple, who are cleaning up the place and tending it. They then recite a hauntingly beautiful poem about

a pair of pine trees that are thought to be wedded to each other. According to this poem, the trees are destined to be together, faithfully, for all eternity. The priest, touched by this poem of fidelity, praises the poem as being more beautiful than anything else he's heard of, on this Earth. The elderly couple then reveal they are, in fact, the spirit of the pines passed down in legend and featured in this poem, and they sail away from the priest in a boat.

Matsukaze (The Wind in the Pines). This tale is about two sisters, called Matsukaze (wind in the pines) and Murasame (autumn rain) who linger in nature and are apparently doomed to linger there, for all time, as a result of their attachment to a former lover. According to Buddhist doctrine, attachment causes misery and so that is the morality of this tale — which is a common theme in Noh.

Sekidera Komachi (Komachi at Seki Temple). This story is about a legendary woman of great beauty, named Komachi. She was renowned for her beauty and literary gifts. This play shows her at the end of her life, when she has come to live in poverty. A priest and some children visit her. The children want her to dance, but she modestly refuses. Once they leave, she is inspired to dance and does so, alone, until dawn, contemplating the transience of living, which once saw her as such a glorious and famous woman, but now a poor old woman living in a hut.

Yorimasa (Warrior Play). This is a classic "warrior" type play, resembling the modern film "Izo" where a famed warrior, in the afterlife, tells his story and asks for a priest to pray for him. In this story, a priest meets an old man. The old man shows him around the local temple and during the course of the tour, the priest notices a fan pattern on the grasses. At last, the old man reveals that he is in fact a famous dead warrior named Minamoto no Yorimasa. He had committed ritual suicide on that spot and the fan pattern is caused by his blood having fanned over that spot, so long ago in the past. In the second half of this play, the warrior, in full armor, relates the details of the battle that took his life, scene by scene. The priest then prays for his soul.

4.1 Classic Japanese Gaming

Another pillar of faith, for us true believers, is the hallowed tradition of Japanese gaming. All-important to the psyche of the true Otaku, we have all learned under the same masters — those great sensei, like Nintendo, Capcom and Square Enix — who taught us all we know about leveling up, racking up on experience and acquiring all the killer moves we need, to beat any level boss that life could throw our way. Yes, a huge percentage of us Japanophiles began to love the culture, through the long hours of intensive initiation we engaged in — controller in hand.

For some of us, myself included, an entire childhood was spent absorbing the ethics of the classic Japanese game, which, subtly perhaps, also educated us concerning the unique Japanese perspective on life — and on such things as ambition, heroism and the way of the warrior. For many of us, this tutelage was a more significant and thorough learning experience than any education we were ever offered by our so-called "real lives."

And so, no Otaku is complete without at least some functional knowledge of this very significant contribution, made by Japan, to the communal consciousness of the Earth, and to Otakus, in particular. Ideally, you should have gone through the mandatory apprenticeship — a childhood of hard-earned experience points and thousands of gaming hours logged. But, at the very least, you must educate yourself on the spirit of classic Japanese gaming, by studying this chapter of the handbook. You can then proceed to make up for lost time, by getting your hands on a decent console and starting a new game, without further ado.

These skills are so important, in fact, that it is the third commandment of the Otaku life. You must know how to handle a controller. If you are a complete newbie, who can't tell the difference between Princess Toadstool and Solid Snake; or if you think "saving your game" involves storing it, safely, in a chest up in the attic, then you've got serious work to do if you want to have any hope of being a true Otaku, within this lifetime. In the hopes of giving you a chance at redemption we will now outline, for you, the history and nature of Japanese classic gaming.

4.2 The History of Japanese Gaming

For gamers, no matter their age, life began in 1973, with the very first Japanese arcade game by legendary video game company, Taito. Beginning with racing and sports games, pioneers and prophets of video gaming, like Taito and Sega soon took control of the burgeoning arcade industry — pushing out American competitors, like Atari and Midway. By the time the "golden age" of arcade gaming began, in 1978, Japan had pretty much dominated the market, with such futures giants of gaming, like Namco Bandai, Nintendo and Konami, joining the competition.

By 1986, console gaming had begun to take hold. Personal gaming consoles had long been available, through American companies like Atari and Coleco. But it wasn't until Japan created their own line of 8 bit gaming consoles — The Nintendo Entertainment System (NES) and the Sega Master System (SMS) — that the console market really took off. As with the arcade market, the all-powerful

prophets of Japanese gaming soon pushed all competitors into the dark mists of obscurity. Atari and Colecovision soon became a laughing stock. The quality and imaginative universes, created by Nintendo and Sega, were so far above anything the competition was doing, that many of the games invented at that time are still popular, such as Legend of Zelda, Final Fantasy, Phantasy Star and Super Mario. In fact, many of the still-popular game franchises, such as Donkey Kong, were created even earlier, in the arcade era of the early 80s.

Two years later, in 1988, Sega and Nintendo upgraded to 16 bit consoles, the Sega Genesis and Super NES, respectively. The largely unsuccessful TurboGrafx 16, produced by Japanese company, NEC, was also released at the same time. The much greater capacity for visual graphics and quality sound really brought classic console gaming into its golden age, and many lush, high quality Square Enix RPGS were launched during this period, such as Secret of Mana, Chrono Trigger, Shining in the Darkness and Shining Force. Soon, the consoles were experimenting with limited 3D gaming and the use of Compact Discs, instead of gaming cartridges. You could buy CD add-ons, to add to your 16-bit system, with the introduction of such CD-based systems as the Genesis Mega Drive.

In 1994, Sony entered the market, with the Sony Playstation (also called the PS1). This was the first popular 32-bit gaming console, and it marked the true conversion to 3D gaming, which is still the norm, today. The 3D capabilities of the Playstation blew away the competition. Atari had tried to re-enter the market, with its Atari Jaguar, but was soon buried by Sony and the other Japanese companies. As with previous ages, the sheer imagination and quality of the Japanese games caused an explosion in video game popularity, which made competition with the Japanese gaming gods virtually impossible. The Playstation operated, for a while, without much competition and during this time it developed highly cinematic games, with an infinitely higher quality of content than ever before. With greater ability to tell stories, this is the time when a lot of the ethics of the Japanese were truly relayed to the gamer nation and so many an Otaku was born. The legendary game

producer, Square Enix, started making unforgettable works of RPG glory, such as Xenogears, Vagrant Story, Star Ocean and the fabled 90s Final Fantasy games. Such cinematic hits as Metal Gear Solid, Resident Evil and Parasite Eve advanced the art of gaming.

Eventually, Nintendo developed a 64-bit console, the Nintendo 64, which threatened to outdo the Playstation. Many of its games, such as Super Mario 64 and The Legend of Zelda: Ocarina of Time, are still considered some of the best games ever produced. In the early 2000s, Microsoft entered the scene, with the technically superior Xbox and provided the first ever viable competition to Japanese gaming, since the beginning. Nintendo and Sony quickly countered, however, with the Nintendo Gamecube and the Playstation 2.

And so began the age of open-ended gaming, in a 3D world. This has led to the explosion of online gaming, personified by such gaming worlds as Assassin's Creed, Call of Duty and Phantasy Star Online. In this new world, Japanese gaming has lost its veritable monopoly, being joined by countries like the USA and France. Both vying to dominate this new market, Japan's Sony and the USA's Microsoft, released the Playstation 3 and the Xbox 360, respectively, in the early 2000s. Both these systems were specifically designed to maximize on the new online gaming craze. They are still competing with each other, today, with the recent release of the Playstation 4 and the Xbox One. Although definitely a contender, now, Microsoft has yet to win a decisive victory against the Japanese gaming industry, which has yet to be uncrowned, as the lords of gaming and the true creators of this thriving industry.

Then — as if to further prove that point — in 2006, Nintendo re-invented the gaming world, yet again, with the introduction of the Nintendo Wii. This system changed all the rules, with its use of motion-detecting gaming paddles and use of peripheral devices, such as the Wii Pad step detector. It was the first gaming system to successfully make use of peripheral devices, to enhance gameplay. Nintendo had been trying to revolutionize gaming, in this way, since the days of the infamous NES Power Glove, but its vision had been too far ahead of technology of the 1980s. With the introduction of

the Wii, the might of the Japanese gaming gods shone through, once more, and revitalized the industry, with such new, imaginative works as WarioWare and the wildly popular fitness game, Wii Fit, which were designed to maximize use of the new peripheral devices. The Wii also appeals to Otaku, everywhere, because of its focus on the classic Japanese gaming franchises, the use of highly creative game design (in the best tradition of the Japanese gaming pioneers) and the heavy reference to manga and anime, through such truly beautiful games as Fragile Dreams, Sakura Wars, Tales of Symphonia, Arc Rise Fantasia and Fire Emblem. These games are basically anime come to life and should appeal to any true-hearted Otaku. What is more, through the innovations of the Wii, the Japanese game designers are continuing that grand tradition of creating compelling, imaginative universes, which has always made them at the forefront of video game evolution.

This brings us, my brethren, to the modern day. If you have read all the above, and taken it to heart, you will have already learned the basics of what you need to know, to fulfill this obligation of true Japanophilia. We have excluded some of the sidestreams of gaming history, such as PC gaming, portable gaming and mobile gaming, but, at least, we have provided a basic education. You will now know, at least, the profound part the Japanese gaming pioneers played, in the creation of modern gaming. Now, it only remains for you to educate yourself on the most popular games and the thriving gaming franchises, which were borne out of the mists of early gaming history. To help you along that path, we will now list them.

4.3 The Main Gaming Franchises

Here, we will list the most popular or enduring gaming franchises, grouped by genre and listed alphabetically. Some games, though not originally created by Japanese companies, are included because of their becoming major institutions, on such Japanese systems as Playstation or Nintendo, or because they were later bought or heavily distributed, by the traditional Japanese gaming companies.

 The Japanophile's Handbook

4.3.1 Action/Adventure

Bomberman

Date Created: 1983.
Company: Hudson Soft.
Invented by: Hudson Soft team.
Most popular games: Bomberman (NES), Bomberman Blast (Wii), Bomberman Land (PS1), Super Bomberman 4 (SNES).
Description: This is a strategic game, where Bomberman plants strategic explosive charges, in order to clear mazes. Beginning in the pre-console days, Bomberman is still popular, spawning an online gaming system, with modern consoles. The best Bomberman experiences, in our experience, are Super Bomberman 4, for the SNES and Bomberman 64, for Nintendo 64.

Castlevania

Date Created: 1986.
Company: Konami.
Invented by: Michel Ancel.
Most popular games: Castlevania(NES), Castlevania 64 (N64), Castlevania: Dracula X (SNES), Castlevania:Lords of Shadow (PS3).
Description: The first popular vampire game, Castlevania has been around since the early NES days. Over the years, it has evolved from a simple bash-em-up action game to much more involved and engrossing cinematic vampire stories. In this case, we recommend the more recent games, rather than the original NES. The recent installments, called Lords of Shadow, are by far the best.

Contra

Date Created: 1987.
Company: Konami.
Invented by: Koji Hiroshita, Shigeharu Umezaki.
Most popular games: Contra (NES), Contra : Hard Corps (Genesis), Neo Contra (PS2), Hard Corps - Uprising (PS3).
Description: This was the best military combat franchise, of much of the early gaming years. It is still a strong franchise, having been updated for PS2 and PS3, in recent years. The best Contra game, in our opinion, is the SNES version, titled Contra III: The Alien Wars.

Crash Bandicoot

Date Created: 1995.
Company: Naughty Dog.
Invented by: Andy Gavin, Jason Rubin.
Most popular games: Crash Bandicoot (PS1), Crash of the Titans (Wii/PS2), Crash Bandicoot: Warped (PS1).
Description Although invented by an American company, this game was produced for exclusive use by Sony and was one of the first popular, original games for the PS1. To learn about this franchise, try getting a hold of any of the original Crash Bandicoot games, for the Playstation 1, which are still considered the best of the series.

Donkey Kong

Date Created: 1981.
Company: Nintendo.
Invented by: Shigeru Miyamoto.
Most popular games: Donkey Kong Country (SNES), Donkey Kong 64 (N64), Donkey Kong (Arcade/NES).
Description This was the game, created by Shigeru Miyamoto, which helped launch the much more successful character of Mario. What is little known, is that Miyamoto had actually wanted to use the Popeye, Bluto and Olive characters, but couldn't get the rights. So, he invented characters with similar roles, Mario, Donkey Kong and a girl named Pauline, who didn't make the cut, it seems, for the Mario games (being replaced by Princess Peach). Although Mario was more successful, Donkey Kong didn't do too badly for himself, either — spawning many games. If you want to familiarize yourself with this topic, you should probably start where it all began — play the antiquated, pixelated version of Donkey Kong, the original game. For more modern examples of quality gaming, try the Donkey Kong Country games, for SNES or Donkey Kong 64, for the Nintendo 64.

Dragon Ball

Date Created: 1986.
Company: Toei Animation.
Invented by: Akira Toriyama.
Most popular games: Dragonball Z: Budokai 3 (PS2), Dragonball Z - Hyper Dimension (SNES), Dragonball Z Retsuden (megadrive).

Description: If you're a fan of the anime, Dragonball Z, then you are in luck! The venerable anime has produced a slew of games, many of which are quite high quality. Beginning with the mediocre Dragon Power, for the NES, in 1986, a great many notable games were later produced. We recommend Dragonball Z: Budokai3, for the Playstation2, as well as Hyper Dimensions, for the SNES.

Frogger

Date Created: 1981.
Company: Konami.
Invented by: Konami team.
Most popular games: Frogger (NES), Frogger 2: Swampy's Revenge (PS1), Frogger Returns (PS3/Wii).
Description: Along with Pac-Man and Q-Bert, Frogger is one of the staples of early arcade gaming. Unlike Q-Bert, however, Frogger is still a thriving franchise. The game originally involved a frog crossing a road, trying not to get killed, but Frogger games have become much more of a gaming universe, and so the later games are better. We suggest you start with Frogger Returns, for the PS3 or Wii or PS1 version of the game, such as Swampy's Revenge.

Gauntlet

Date Created: 1985.
Company: Tengen, Midway Games.
Invented by: Tengen and Midway teams.
Most popular games: Gauntlet: Dark Legacy (PS2, Gamecube), Gauntlet (NES), Gauntlet Legends (PS1, N64).
Description: This game invented the sword and sorcery "dungeon crawl" genre. It has lasted since the pre-console days and is still going strong, as a franchise. A collaboration between Japanese Tengen and American Midway, the best games in the franchise include Dark Legacy, for PS2 and Gauntlet Legends, for PS1.

Ghost and Goblins

Date Created: 1985.
Company: Capcom.
Invented by: Tokuro Fujiwara.
Most popular games: Ghouls and Ghosts (Genesis), Ghosts and Goblins (NES), Gargoyle's Quest (Gameboy).

Description: The iconic early master of gothic atmosphere, the Ghosts and Goblins franchise was the precursor to all future macabre, horror-based games. Although not very scary, given the limits of the early technology, it definitely nailed the spooky atmosphere. The best examples of this franchise are Ghouls and Ghosts, for Genesis, or Gargoyle's Quest, which was a spin-off, following the adventures of a Gargoyle, rather than the armor-clad knight, who usually served as the series' protagonist.

Golden Axe

Date Created: 1989.
Company: Sega.
Invented by: Makoto Uchida.
Most popular games: Golden Axe (Genesis), Golden Axe 2 (Genesis), Golden Axe: Beast Rider (PS3).
Description: This is the most popular sword and sorcery, barbarian epic game in the history of gaming, Golden Axe has relatively few games, but is still being produced and is a cult classic among Otaku. You will often find a Genesis set up, at anime festivals, for true gamers to enjoy a game of Golden Axe. The only way to experience this series is by playing 1 or 2, on the original Genesis system.

Kid Icarus

Date Created: 1986.
Company: Nintendo.
Invented by: Satoru Okada.
Most popular games: Kid Icarus (NES), Kid Icarus Uprising (Nindendo 3DS), Kid Icarus Remake (Wii).
Description: This game was made by Nintendo, at the same time as Metroid. It is suggested the student of gaming try both Kid Icarus and Metroid, on the NES and observe their similarities. It follows the adventures of an angel named Icarus. Although Metroid did much better, Kid Icarus saw many portable Game Boy games and the original title was remade, in 2007, for the Wii Console.

Kirby

Date Created: 1992.
Company: Nintendo.
Invented by: Masahiro Sakurai.

<u>Most popular games:</u> Kirby's Adventure (NES), Kirby's Return to Dreamland (Wii), Kirby 64: The Crystal Shards (N64).

<u>Description:</u> The last real hit character to be created for the NES, Kirby has since become one of the favorite mascots for Nintendo. Kirby is a cute pink ball-like creature, who inflates like a balloon and floats. The best Kirby games, in our opinion, are Kirby's Return to Dreamland, for Wii, and the original NES game, Kirby's Adventure.

Legend of Zelda

<u>Date Created:</u> 1986.

<u>Company:</u> Nintendo.

<u>Invented by:</u> Shigeru Miyamoto, Takashi Tezuka.

<u>Most popular games:</u> Legend of Zelda: An Ocarina in Time (N64), Legend of Zelda: A Link to the Past (SNES), Adventures of Link (NES), Legend of Zelda: Twilight Princess (Wii).

<u>Description</u> Another of Nintendo's giants, this franchise has spawned 17 games, to date, which have spanned all of Nintendo's consoles, since the beginning. It is a high fantasy adventure RPG series, which focus on the main character, named Link. To start an education on the Zelda franchise, you could try some of the latest games, which really highlight the Zelda universe, with truly cinematic Wii-level graphics. Twilight Princess is a good choice. Or you could examine the history of the universe more closely, by checking out A Link to the Past. However, our first recommendation, by far, is that you play An Ocarina in Time, for the Nintendo 64, as it is the best Zelda game ever produced.

Mario

<u>Date Created:</u> 1981.

<u>Company:</u> Nintendo.

<u>Invented by:</u> Shigeru Miyamoto.

<u>Most popular games:</u> Super Mario Bros (NES), Super Mario Galaxy (Wii), Paper Mario(Wii), Super Mario 64(N64), Super Mario World(SNES).

<u>Description</u> The best-selling video game franchise of all time, Mario was invented by Nintendo game designer Shigeru Miyamoto and first appeared in the Nintendo game "Donkey Kong" in 1981. Mario became popular with the game Super Mario Bros., which was released on the NES, in 1986. It is popular not only for the imaginative universe of Mario, but also for its music, famously written by Koji Kondo.

Mario has a brother, named Luigi, and friends, such as Princess
Peach(or Toadstool), Toad (a mushroom man) and Yoshi (a ridable
dragon). There are various villains in Mario games, including Bowser (a
lizardlike thing), Wario (the evil anti-Mario) and Donkey Kong (a
gorilla). To introduce yourself to Mario games, try beginning with any
"Super Mario" game, Paper Mario or Mario RPG.

Mega Man

Date Created: 1987.
Company: Capcom.
Invented by: Akira Kitamura.
Most popular games: Megaman II (NES), Mega Man X4 (Saturn/PS1),
Mega Man 6 (NES).
Description: Reminiscent of the anime, Astroboy, Mega Man is the
story of an inventor (Dr. Light) who invents Mega Man, to be his hero
in the battle against evil inventor, Dr. Wily. Dr. Wily creates a series of
evil robots, which Mega Man must fight. Another staple of gaming lore,
the most memorable Mega Man games, in our view, are the long series
of NES games. However, Mega Man X4, for playstation, is also
memorable.

Metal Gear Solid

Date Created: 1998.
Company: Konami.
Created by: Hideo Kojima, Motoyuki Yoshioka.
Most popular games: Metal Gear Solid (PS1), Metal Gear Rising:
Revengeance (PS3), Metal Gear Solid: Snake Eater (PS2).
Description: The first real "tactical espionage" game, featuring famous
game protagonist, Solid Snake, this Konami game started with the game
Metal Gear Solid, for PS1, in 1996. It was actually based on an earlier,
far less complicated game, called Metal Gear, for the NES. In creating
this game, Konami invented a new, exciting genre, that lets the gamer
engage in dangerous espionage missions. To start, we greatly
recommend the original game, Metal Gear Solid, for the PS1. It is the
only way to learn the history.

Metroid

Date Created: 1986.
Company: Nintendo.

<u>Invented by:</u> Makoto Kano, Gunpei Yokoi, Hiroji Kiyotake.
<u>Most popular games:</u> Metroid (NES), Super Metroid (SNES), Metroid
Prime (Wii/Gamecube), Metroid Prime 2(Wii/Gamecube).
<u>Description:</u> One of the classics of vintage NES gaming, Metroid is still
a thriving and wildly popular franchise, which is rumored to be made
into a live-action film, in the near future. It is famous for having a
female protagonist, Samus, who inhabits a sci-fi world, where metroids
(jellyfish-like creatures) abound. For beginners, we highly recommend
Super Metroid for the Super Nintendo.

Ninja Gaiden

<u>Date Created:</u> 1988.
<u>Company:</u> Tecmo.
<u>Invented by:</u> Hideo Yoshizawa, Tomonobu Itagaki.
<u>Most popular games:</u> Ninja Gaiden (NES), Ninja Gaiden Sigma (PS3),
Ninja Gaiden Remake (Xbox).
<u>Description:</u> Along with Shinobi, this is the definitive ninja series of
early gaming history. Ninja Gaiden was famed for its cinematics, at a
time when early NES games were not very cinematic. It is
recommended you check out the early NES series and the new Ninja
Gaiden Sigma series, for PS3.

Pac-Man

<u>Date Created:</u> 1980.
<u>Company:</u> Namco Bandai.
<u>Invented by:</u> Toru Iwatani.
<u>Most popular games:</u> Pac-Man(Arcade/NES), Pac-Man World (PS1),
Pac-Mania (NES), Pac-Man World 2 (PS2).
<u>Description:</u> The original iconic Arcade game, Pac-Man was invented
by Japanese company Namco, a branch of Bandai Entertainment (of
anime fame). The game has been popular, ever since the early days of
gaming and it still a popular character. If you never played the original
Pac-Man, then what rock did you crawl out from under? You simply
can't be an Otaku without having played the original Pac-Man — so
hop to it! Pac-Man World and Pac-Man World 2, for the PS1 and PS2
are also memorable entries.

Pitfall

<u>Date Created:</u> 1987.

<u>Company:</u> Activision.
<u>Invented by:</u> David Crane.
<u>Most popular games:</u> Super Pitfall (NES), Pitfall: The Mayan Adventure (SNES/Genesis), Pitfall 3D: Beyond the Jungle (PS1).
<u>Description:</u> Developed by Activision, this is one of the few Atari games to produce a thriving franchise. In the original game, an explorer runs and jumps through the jungle, avoiding pitfalls. We suggest the PS1 title, Pitfall 3D, as the best example of a Pitfall game.

Pokemon

<u>Date Created:</u> 1987.
<u>Company:</u> Sega.
<u>Invented by:</u> Yutaka Sugano.
<u>Most popular games:</u> Hey You, Pikachu! (N64), Pokemon Emerald (Game Boy Advance), Pokemon Fire Red (Game Boy Advance).
<u>Description:</u> Unlike most anime, Pokemon was inspired by a video game, rather than starting — like most anime — with a manga. And these "Pikachu games" were just as popular as the anime. There are endless Pokemon games. If you want to educate yourself on Pokemon, it is actually recommended you examine the original Game Boy games, which launched the franchise. The N64 monster-raising engine is also memorable.

Rayman

<u>Date Created:</u> 1995.
<u>Company:</u> Ubisoft.
<u>Invented by:</u> Michel Ancel.
<u>Most popular games:</u> Rayman 2 (PS1/N64), Rayman Legends (Wii), Rayman (PS1), Rayman 3: Hoodlum Havoc (PS2).
<u>Description:</u> Created by Ubisoft, a French game designer, Rayman is one of the few early French hits. Rayman began on the PS1, in 1995, and has since produced many popular titles, including the most recent Rayman Legends. We recommend that title, as well as the original PS1 game, for those who wish to learn about Rayman.

Resident Evil

<u>Date Created:</u> 1996.
Company: Capcom.
<u>Invented by:</u> Shinji Mikami.

Most popular games: Resident Evil (PS1), Resident Evil: Code Veronica (PS2), Resident Evil 4 (Gamecube).

Description Resident Evil was one of the breakthrough games for Playstation, when the PS1 first came out. It helped create the new genre of realistic 3D survival horror games, along with Parasite Eve. Until the PS1 came along, this genre was not credibly possible. It has continued to the present day, producing 23 games and branching out into live-action films, animation and action figures. To start with, we greatly recommend getting a copy of the first game, which is still one of the best. Or, better yet, play the 2002 remake of the original game, for Gamecube, Wii or PS3.

Shinobi

Date Created: 1987.
Company: Sega.
Invented by: Yutaka Sugano.
Most popular games: Shinobi (SMS), Revenge of Shinobi (Genesis), Shinobi (PS2), Shadow Dancer: The Secret of Shinobi(Genesis).
Description: Whereas Ninja Gaiden was the main ninja game for NES, Shinobi was the main ninja game for Sega consoles. It is strongly recommended you start with Revenge of Shinobi, if you want to learn about Shinobi. In our opinion, it is the best and most atmospheric Shinobi game, with the most memorable score. Shadow Dancer, for Genesis, was also unique for its gameplay.

Sonic

Date Created: 1991.
Company: Sega.
Invented by: Naoto Ohshima, Yuji Naka.
Most popular games: Sonic the Hedgehog (Genesis), Sonic Adventure 2 (Gamecube), Sonic and Knuckles (Genesis).
Description One of Sega's most memorable franchises, Sonic the Hedgehog has been ported into practically every gaming system that ever existed. It has been made into innumerable other tv shows, PC games and comic books. It began with the Sega Genesis game, Sonic the Hedgehog, which was released in 1991. At the time, it was revolutionary for its fast action and compelling world. To introduce yourself to Sonic, try playing the original Sonic the Hedgehog 1 or 2 or find a version of Sonic Adventure.

Spyro

Date Created: 1998.
Company: Insomniac Games.
Invented by: Mark Cerny, Alex Hastings, Brian Hastings, Ted Price.
Most popular games: Spyro the Dragon (PS1), The Legend of Spyro: A New Beginning (PS2, Gamecube), The Legend of Spyro: Dawn of the Dragon (PS3, Wii), Spyro: A Hero's Tail (PS2).
Description: Another American invention, Spyro was associated closely with the Playstation, for much of its history. It was the PS1, in 1998, which first made Spyro popular. Spyro is a little, tough and wise-cracking dragon who explores a 3D dragon world. We suggest the original playstation games, to get an idea of this game franchise.

Strider

Date Created: 1989.
Company: Capcom.
Invented by: Kouichi Yotsui.
Most popular games: Strider (Genesis), Strider (PS3), Strider 2(PS1).
Description: One of Capcom's early successes, Strider takes place in a science fiction setting, in Russia. The main character battles the machines of a highly technological Russia, using stealth and amazing acrobatics. It gets extra Otaku props for being based on a manga, called Strider Hiryu. We recommend the reboot of the original Genesis game, which was released in 2014, for the Playstation 3.

Tomb Raider

Date Created: 1996.
Company: Core Design.
Invented by: Core Design Team.
Most popular games: Tomb Raider (PS1), Tomb Raider II (PS1), Tomb Raider (remake) (PS3).
Description: Invented by a British company, it follows the adventure of British Archeologist, Lara Croft. She's like a female version of Indiana Jones, but much hotter. The game was launched in 1996, on the Playstation 1 and Sega Saturn. It has since spawned feature films, comic books and a great many other spin-off products. Begin your tomb raiding by playing either the original PS1 game, or the 2010 remake, for the PS3.

 **The Japanophile's Handbook**

4.3.2 Fighting/Sports

Double Dragon

Date Created: 1987.
Company: Technos Japan.
Invented by: Yoshihisa Kishimoto.
Most popular games: Double Dragon (NES/SMS), Double Dragon II (NES), Double Dragon Neon (PS3).
Description: Before there was Street Fighter, Mortal Kombat or Tekken, Double Dragon was the ultimate fighting game and it really helped to define the genre. It was recently resurrected in PS3 form, with Double Dragon Neon. However, it is recommended the curious try Double Dragon II, for the NES, to really get an idea of why this franchise was so successful and so playable.

Gran Turismo

Date Created: 1997.
Company: Sony.
Invented by: Kanunori Yamauchi.
Most popular games: Gran Turismo (PS1), Gran Turismo 3: A-spec(PS2), Gran Turismo 6 (PS3).
Description: This game was the definition of quality car racing, since the beginning of Playstation gaming. Developed by Sony, in 1997, it provides the most realistic portrayal of racing, in our opinion, and should satisfy any lover of racing games. Any game in the series will do, but it is worth checking out the newest installment, if you want to see the cutting edge of game racing.

Mortal Kombat

Date Created: 1992.
Company: Midway Games.
Invented by: Ed Boon, John Tobias.
Most popular games: Mortal Kombat (Genesis), Mortal Kombat: Deception (PS2, Gamecube), Mortal Kombat 4 (N64).
Description: Created by early American arcade game company, Midway Games, this is one of the few run-away hits created by early Japanese gaming's competition. We believe it was their answer to the popularity of Street Fighter, and did just as well as its competitor. We recommend

either Mortal Kombat: Deception, for PS2 or Mortal Kombat 4, for the Nintendo 64, if you can get it.

Samurai Showdown

Date Created: 1993.
Company: SNK.
Invented by: SNK team.
Most popular games: Samurai Showdown (SNES), Samurai Showdown 3 (PS1), Samurai Showdown Anthology (PS2).
Description: Based in 18th century Japan, this is an all-samurai version of Street Fighter. Beginning on the SNES, in 1993, Samurai Showdown is still an active franchise. For beginners, we definitely recommend Samurai Showdown 3, as being the best of them all.

Street Fighter

Date Created: 1987.
Company: Capcom.
Invented by: Takashi Nishiyama, Hiroshi Matsumoto.
Most popular games: Street Fighter 2 (SNES), Street Fighter Alpha 3 (PS1/Dreamcast), Super Street Fighter IV (PS3).
Description: The most iconic of all fighting games, Street Fighter was first popularized by the creation of Street Fighter II, for the SNES and Genesis systems, in the early 90s. The game has spawned movies, comics and many other spin-off products. We recommend all the games in the series, but playing Street Fighter II — the original game, with its original 11 characters — will give you the best idea about how Street Fighter mania first began.

Super Smash Bros

Date Created: 1999.
Company: Nintendo.
Invented by: Masahiro Sakurai.
Most popular games: Super Smash Bros (N64), Super Smash Bros: Melee (Gamecube), Super Smash Bros: Brawl (Wii).
Description: This is a crossover game, which lets you fight other characters. All fighting characters in the game are famous Nintendo mascots, such as Mario, Kirby or Metroid. It is basically a Nintendo character fighting game! Very popular among Otaku, most anime

festivals include a competitive Super Smash Bros. tournament, so all Otakus should learn how to play the game. Any version will do.

Tekken

Date Created: 1994.
Company: Namco Bandai.
Invented by: Namco Bandai Team.
Most popular games: Tekken (PS1), Tekken Tag Tournament (PS2), Tekken 6 (PS3), Tekken 3 (PS1).
Description: This is a 3D fighting game, created by Namco Bandai Entertainment, which was the first to really take advantage of the new 3D technology of the PS1. It has developed, since then, to spawn many games, and many spin-off titles and action films. The best place to start is Tekken 3, for the PS1, which we consider to be one of the best for gameplay, story and cinematics.

Tony Hawk

Date Created: 1998.
Company: Namco Bandai.
Invented by: Namco Bandai team.
Most popular games: Tony Hawk Pro Skater 3 (PS2), Tony Hawk Pro Skater (PS1), Tony Hawk's Underground (PS2).
Description: This was the most popular sports games, in the early history of Playstation. With skateboarding, BMX biking and the like, this game was the first to fully utilize the new 3D powers of the newer generation of consoles. Although, sadly, discontinued, it's recommended avid games try at least one Tony Hawk game.

Virtua Fighter

Date Created: 1993.
Company: Sega.
Invented by: Sega team.
Most popular games: Virtua Fighter (Arcade/Saturn), Virtua Fighter 2 (Arcade/Genesis), Virtua Fighter 4 (PS2).
Description: Although not as popular as Tekken, Virtua Fighter,

invented by Sega, in 1993, has the distinction of being the very first 3D fighting game and so defined a new genre. The uninitiated might want to check out Virtua Fighter 2 or 4, the best games.

The Japanophile's Handbook

4.3.3 Strategy/RPG/Simulation/Puzzle

Arc the Lad

Date Created: 1995.
Company: Sony.
Invented by: Sony team.
Most popular games: Arc the Lad II (PS1), Arc the Lad I (PS1).
Description: This is a tactical RPG which became very popular and
spawned a quality anime series of the same name. It follows the
adventures of Arc in a fantasy world as he battles monsters, seeks to
find his father and discover the destiny of his home world. Popular
opinion suggests that II is, by far, the best game, but it's recommended
you start from the beginning, because the story is linear, between
games.

Chrono Series

Date Created: 1995.
Company: Square Enix.
Invented by: Square Enix team.
Most popular games: Chrono Trigger (PS1), Chrono Break (PS2).
Description: This is a quality RPG series, made by quality game
designers, Square Enix. It began with time-travelling RPG Chrono
Trigger, for the Playstation 1. Those who wish to educate themselves
on the Chrono series are recommended to start at the beginning, for
Chrono Trigger is often called, by some people, one of the best RPGs
ever made.

Digimon

Date Created: 1998.
Company: Namco Bandai.
Invented by: Namco Bandai team.
Most popular games: Digimon World (PS1), Digimon World Data
Squad (PS2), Digimon World 3 (PS1).
Description: This well-known children's anime has also been a huge
success in the gaming world. Being a Monster Trainer genre of anime,
Digimon translates well into video game form. For a great example of
this monster-raising franchise, try the original Digimon World, for PS1,
or one of the Playstation sequels.

Dragon Quest

Date Created: 1986.
Company: Chunsoft.
Invented by: Koichi Nakamura.
Most popular games: Dragon Warrior (NES), Dragon Warrior II (NES), Dragon Quest VI (SNES).
Description: This is the most venerable of popular RPGS! Starting with Dragon Warrior, for the NES, in 1986, the Dragon Quest series defined the genre, with a hero, a villain, a quest, pacing NPCs, and endless monsters to fight. It also inspired manga, novels and anime, and so it is highly recommended all aspiring Otaku get to know this game franchise. A good place to start is either with the very first NES game or with Dragon Quest VI for the SNES.

Final Fantasy

Date Created: 1987.
Company: Square Enix.
Invented by: Hironobu Sakaguchi.
Most popular games: Final Fantasy VI (SNES), Final Fantasy X (PS2), Final Fantasy IX (PS1), Final Fantasy Tactics (PS1).
Description: This is the absolute definitive RPG, out of them all! Final Fantasy is the most deeply respected cinematic, anime-style gaming institution there is, and no Otaku is complete without a knowledge of this franchise's long and storied history. And it all began with a humble NES game, in 1987. It takes place in a thoroughly unique world, which needs to be experienced, in order to understand. Luckily for us all, the Final Fantasy games are still being produced, without a sign of stopping. We suggest you start either with the most recent Final Fantasy or with one of the legendary canon of 1990s Final Fantasy games, which have developed something of a cult following, among ardent gamers.

Harvest Moon

Date Created: 1996.
Company: Marvelous Interactive.
Invented by: Yasuhiro Wada.
Most popular games: Harvest Moon 64 (N64), Harvest Moon: A Wonderful Life (Gamecube), Rune Factory 4 (Nintendo DS).

Description: This is an interesting mix of a strategy game, a simulation and an anime RPG. You are a cute anime-like farmer, who has to buy chickens, grow crops, participate in local events, make friends, build a house and woo a bride. It is, basically, a fascinating concept. The best game, in our opinion, is the Nintendo 64 version, which was the first to take full advantage of the new 3D.

Koei Strategy Games

Date Created: 1978.
Company: Koei.
Invented by: Yoichi Erikawa, Keiko Erikawa.
Most popular games: Romance of the Three Kingdoms (NES/SNES), Ghenghis Khan (NES/SNES), Nobunaga's Ambition (NES/SNES), Bandit Kings of Ancient China (NES).
Description: This entry has to do with the work of an entire video game company, Koei. They were the defining force behind historical simulation games, in the early days. They tended to focus on historically accurate military strategy, in a variety of historical eras, but they also did historically accurate adventure games, such as Uncharted Waters and Inindo (a ninja RPG). Some of their franchises, such as Romance of the Three Kingdoms, have become legendary, and are still remade, on modern gaming systems. We recommend this title, as the perfect introduction to Koei games.

Mana Series

Date Created: 1991.
Company: Square Enix.
Invented by: Koichi Ishii.
Most popular games: Secret of Mana (SNES), Legend of Mana (PS1), Dawn of Mana (PS2).
Description: Another quality RPG by Square Enix, this one goes all the way back to the 1991 SNES game, Secret of Mana. For beginners, we strongly recommend this game, as a starting point. Although the game which preceded the Mana series, and served as the inspiration, is also good. It is called Final Fantasy Adventure.

Maxis Simulations

Date Created: 1987.
Company: Maxis, Electronic Arts.

<u>Invented by:</u> Will Wright.
<u>Most popular games:</u> Sim City (SNES), Sim City 2000 (N64), Sim City 2000 (Sega Saturn), Sim City 2000 (PS2).
<u>Description:</u> This entry has to do with the work of a video game company, rather than a single game. All simulations, apart from historical ones (ruled by Koei) were absolutely defined by Maxis, an American company. Maxis was first popularized by the game Sim City, for the Super Nintendo. It was bought by EA, in 1997, and other popular games were created, such as the still popular game, The Sims, which was first ported to the PS2 and Gamecube consoles. We suggest playing both Sim City and The Sims, if you want to get an idea of the magic of Maxis games.

Monster Rancher

<u>Date Created:</u> 1997.
<u>Company:</u> Tecmo Koei.
<u>Invented by:</u> Tecmo Koei team.
<u>Most popular games:</u> Monster Rancher (PS1), Monster Rancher 2 (PS1), Monster Rancher 4 (PS2).
<u>Description:</u> This series is probably the most well-done of the Monster Battle genre games. If you like really interesting, compelling and challenging monster training games, with a real richness of characters and possibilities, then Monster Rancher is for you. Those who want to start off with this game are advised to begin with either 4, for PS2, or the original, for PS1.

Phantasy Star

<u>Date Created:</u> 1987.
<u>Company:</u> Sega.
<u>Invented by:</u> Kotaro Hayashida, Miki Morimoto.
<u>Most popular games:</u> Phantasy Star (SMS), Phantasy Star II (Genesis), Phantasy Star IV (Genesis).
<u>Description:</u> The greatest RPG to ever be produced by Sega, it was first introduced in 1987, on the Sega Master System. Phantasy Star is a Science Fantasy game, taking place in a future of space travel and high technological achievement. The franchise is popular with Otaku, because of the consistently anime style of the cinematics. For beginners, the original Phantasy Star, for SMS and Phantasy Star IV, for Genesis, are the finest artifacts of this franchise. This series inspired the creation

of Phantasy Star Online, one of the first popular online gaming systems to gain a following.

Star Ocean

Date Created: 1996.
Company: Square Enix.
Invented by: Yoshiharu Gotanda.
Most popular games: Star Ocean: The Second Story (PS1), Star Ocean: Till the End of Time (PS2), Star Ocean: Last Hope (PS3).
Description: Not as well-known as some other Square Enix titles, we personally find this series remarkably innovative. It takes the classic RPG into new ground, with cooking competitions, user-driven romantic subplots and other such features, which give a subtle nod to anime themes, which any true Otaku will understand. The style is consistently anime. For an example of Star Ocean's appeal, try Star Ocean: The Second Story, for the Playstation 1.

Tales Series

Date Created: 1995.
Company: Namco Bandai.
Invented by: Yoshiharu Gotanda.
Most popular games: Tales of Symphonia (Gamecube), Tales of the Abyss (PS2), Tales of Vesperia (PS3).

Description: The Tales series is another masterpiece of fantasy RPG games, this time, however, not produced by Square Enix. This one was made by Namco Bandai, and has an ever-growing list of high quality games. With a beautiful anime style and compelling, well-made characters and stories, this series has a strong following among Otaku. We recommend you try Tales of Symphonia, for Gamecube, or Tales of the Vesperia, for PS3.

Tetris

Date Created: 1984.
Company: Various, mostly Nintendo.
Invented by: Alexey Pajitnov.
Most popular games: Tengen Tetris (NES), Tetris Party (Wii), The New Tetris (N64), Tetris Attack (SNES).

Description: The only major franchise created by a Russian, tetris was designed by a Soviet game designer, Alexey Pajitinov. It was sold to various gaming companies, including Nintendo, who ported it to the NES, in 1986. It is, arguably, the most popular puzzle game in the world. Although many versions have been made, any of them are suitable to help the gamer quickly learn how Tetris works.

Wizardry

Date Created: 1981.
Company: Sir-Tech.
Invented by: Andrew Greenberg, Robert Woodhead.
Most popular games: Wizardry: Proving Grounds of the Mad Overlord (NES), Wizardry 6: Bane of the Cosmic Forge (SNES).
Description: This RPG is the best dungeon-based gaming franchise ever produced. Hardcore lovers of RPG and Dungeons-and-Dragons-like gaming systems will absolutely live for this franchise. It is sword and sorcery, distilled, and at its very best. The best installments are either number VI or VII, both for the SNES.

5.1 Japanese Culture

If you've diligently studied all the previous chapters, you should be well on your way to legitimate Otakuhood. But you're not quite there yet. By following the three commandments, already laid out, you may have already built yourself a sturdy foundation, but you will never make that leap into true Japanophile glory until you've completely learned the most important lesson of all: a genuine understanding of the Japanese culture. This is the fourth commandment — possibly the most important commandment of all. You need to have an authentic insight into the culture — unsullied by the distortions of anime, manga and popular culture — in order to be a true connoisseur of all things Japanese. You need to literally be able to realistically walk down a street in the Shibuya shopping district of Tokyo and thoroughly understand what you're seeing: every conventional act of etiquette you may see between pedestrians; every strange and exotic food item you may see for sale in the marketplace; every cultural reference you see on the TV screen as you pass by the video billboards. Although gaps are permissible (as even the Japanese may be unaware of a few things) you, at the very least, need to know the prevailing etiquette and — most importantly — what is expected from a foreigner.

Indeed, when armed with this knowledge, you can effectively drive away the ugly specter of the Weeaboo, for good and all. Because, by

far, the most defining characteristic of the Weeaboo is a fundamental ignorance of what Japanese culture actually is. They base all their knowledge on what they've learned from anime, popular American movies or video games, which were set in Japan, and so they completely misunderstand the culture. This is why they have such a tendency to make fools of themselves, in front of Japanese people and Otakus alike. To avoid this horrible fate and leave the perils of Weeaboo behavior behind you, forever, study the all-important cultural information, presented in this chapter. And, don't stop there. Although we give you the basic cliff notes, here, which will point you in the right direction, you need to be willing to delve further into these topics and really study hard. You must look upon your scholarship into the nature of Japanese culture as a lifelong education. More than anything — more than anime or film or Kabuki theatre — this is the most important field of education you have to pursue, to make yourself acceptable and likeable to the Japanese people, themselves. And, given we're all Japanophiles here, what is more important than that?

5.2 The Japanese Language

Any self-respecting Japanophile should, at the very least, know the difference between kanji and kana, as well as a few choice phrases. If, for no other reason, than to be able to catch the occasional word or phrase, in your favorite anime, without having to read the subtitles. Although teaching you Japanese falls outside the scope of this book, true Japanophiles are encouraged to study the language, as fluent Japanese is one of the most promising ways of fulfilling all your Japanophile dreams — given that it may, theoretically, allow you to visit Japan and "blend in", so to speak. At least as much as it is possible for a foreigner to do so. However, for this book, we will just give you basic information, which constitutes the bare minimum of what any Japanophile should know about the language, so that the less studious, among us, can do a bit of catching up.

To start, you should understand the types of Japanese writing systems. Unlike most languages, Japanese has more than one system for expressing words and ideas. The main system is called kanji, and is adopted from the ancient Chinese ideographic script. A kanji

character will look like the diagram, below, and is different from Roman letters, in that each individual kanji character represents an idea, rather than a syllable. For example, the kanji characters, below, represent "destiny", "honor" and "harmony."

命	誉	和
Destiny	**Honor**	**Harmony**

In addition to kanji, there are the phonetic writing systems, called the kana scripts. These characters function like Roman alphabet characters, in that they represent sounds. They are divided into two types, Hiragana, which is used to phonetically spell out Japanese words, and Katakana, which is used to phonetically spell out foreign words, or words borrowed or adapted from other languages. A lot of Japanese sentences will be a mixture of Kanji, Katakana and Hiragana. Given this mix, and the fact that Kanji has over 2,000 characters, Japanese is considered one of the hardest languages in the world to learn. Now, maybe you can see why we don't endeavor to teach it here. It's a lot more complicated than learning your ABCs. However, the ambitious Japanophile is encouraged to, at least, learn common kanji characters and learn to read hiragana, which often spells out easily understandable western words.

ハンバーガー	カリフォルニフ
Hiragana for "Hamburger"	**Katakana for "California"**

 **The Japanophile's Handbook**

In addition, some knowledge of conversational Japanese is recommended, since the Japanese language, in spoken form, is considerably less complicated than its written form. And so, becoming fluent in spoken Japanese is a much more easily attainable dream. Once again, teaching you Japanese vocabulary falls outside the scope of this handbook, since it is not an absolute requirement for living a Japanophile life. But, we'll list some of the most useful and popular Japanese phrases, in the diagram, on next page, just to give you a taste of the language and to help you find the bathrooms, if you're ever in Shibuya Station.

COMMON / USEFUL JAPANESE PHRASES

Where is the bathroom?	Toire wa doko desuka?
Thank you!	Arigatou!
Good morning!	Ohayo Gozaimasu!
Good evening!	Konbanwa!
How are you?	Ogenki desuka?
I'm fine.	Watashi wa genki desu.
Hello!	Konnichiwa! (time specific greetings are preferred).
Hello! (over phone)	Moshi moshi!
Goodbye!	Sayonara!
See you later!	Mata atode aimashou!
Good night!	Oyasumi nasai!
Sorry.	Gomenasai.
Do you speak English?	Anata wa eigo wo hanashimasu ka?
What's your name?	Namae wa nandesu ka?
My name is...	Watashi no namae wa...
Nice to meet you!	Hajimemashite!
I speak little Japanese.	Watashi ha nihongo ga sukosi dake hanasemasu.
I like Japanese people!	Watashi wa nihongo ga suki desu!

5.3 Japanese Food

And now, in the best tradition of the cooking genre manga series, we'll all salivate about the various kinds of delightful foods invented by the Japanese. Japan's cuisine is unique and distinctive from any other form of cuisine in the world. Most people, if presented with a Japanese dish, will be able to detect both the esthetics and the ingredients which make the dish distinctly Japanese. But, for the true, red-blooded Japanophile this is not enough. All true blue Otaku should desire to become so aware of the Japanese culinary arts that they can tell the difference between a Soba noodle and a Udon noodle, while blind-folded. You don't have to learn to like Natto, but you should, at least, be able to differentiate Sushi from Sashimi. After all, learning about the food is probably the most enjoyable and appetizing part of the entire Japanophile experience. In the hopes of educating the unenlightened, we will now list the majority of Japan's national dishes, from Agedashi Dofu to Zoni.

# The Japanophile's Handbook

Agedashi Dofu

This is a way to serve hot tofu. Silken firm tofu, cut into cubes, is lightly dusted with potato or corn starch and deep fried until brown. It is served in hot tentsuyu broth, which is made from dashi, mirin and soy sauce. It is usually topped with finely chopped spring onion or dried bonito flakes.

Chawanmushi

This is an egg custard dish. It consists of an egg mixture flavored with mirin, dashi and soya sauce. Other ingredients can be mixed with it, such as shiitake mushrooms, gingko and boiled shrimp. This is one of the few Japanese dishes that must be eaten with a spoon. It is usually eaten in a bowl, as a quick meal.

Chankonabe

This is a dish traditionally eaten by sumo wrestlers, in order to help build muscle and gain weight, in a relatively healthy way. But it has become popular with the public. Retired sumo wrestlers often open restaurants, specializing in the dish. It contains a dashi or chicken broth soup base with mirin or sake, added for flavor. Typically, all kind of foods are added to Chankonabe, to augment it, but they are typically high protein foods, such as chicken, fish, tofu, beef or daikon and bok choy.

Chirashizushi

This is "scattered sushi", basically a bowl of sushi rice, topped with any kind of topping you would normally find on sushi. Toppings are up to the chef or the diner. There are, however, generally three types: edomae chirashizushi (Edo style), which is uncooked ingredients, arranged artfully; gomokuzushi (Kansai style), which can have both cooked and uncooked ingredients, which are all mixed together; and sake-zushi (Kyushu style) where rice wine is used, and is topped with shrimp, sea bream, octopus, shiitake mushroom or bamboo shoots.

Chikuzenni

This is a dish that originated from northern Kyushi. It consists of braised chicken and vegetables, seasoned with dashi, mirin or shiitake flavored seasoning. It is often eaten when bringing in the new year in Japan.

Dango

This is a kind of dumpling made from rice flour, similar to mochi. It is often served with green tea and comes in many flavors. Certain varieties are usually served at certain seasons of the year. Dango dumplings are often served on skewers.

Edamame

These are immature soybeans, still in their pod. They are generally boiled or steamed in lightly salted water. They are also found in Chinese, Korean and Hawaiian food, but are more heavily salted.

Fugu

This is the Japanese word for pufferfish. The pufferfish contains a toxic poison, but the ancient Japanese chefs discovered that the rest of the fish was delicious, so it has become a delicacy, in Japan. Fugu preparation is strictly controlled, in Japan, in order to avoid accidents. It is generally served raw, like sashimi.

Goya Chanpuru

Chanpuru is a kind of Okinawan stir-fry. Goya Chanpuru is a stir-fry of bitter lemon, tofu, egg and sliced pork.

Himono

Also called Sakano no Himono, this is a kind of popular breakfast food,

consisting of dried fish. There are many kinds, ranging from mackerel to sardine, to pike or barracuda.

Ikayaki

A popular fast food, it is basically grilled squid topped with soya sauce. Ikayaki is served at many drinking establishments and is often accompanied by alcoholic drinks. They are also popular at festivals.

Inarizushi

This is a kind of sushi. But instead of being rolled or topped with ingredients, inarizushi involves a pouch of fried tofu, which is stuffed with sushi rice. It is named after our favorite Shinto god, Inari, who is believed to have a fondness for fried tofu. There is a Hawaiian variant of this sushi, which includes various vegetables, fried in a triangular pouch, made of deep fried tofu.

Kaiseki

This is a traditional style of dinner, which has many courses. It is a very artistic affair, in that aesthetics are as important as the taste of the dish, itself. There are two types of kaiseki: the kind called simply kaiseki, refers to a set menu of carefully selected foods, served on individual trays; and the more specialized kaiseki-ryori, is a simple meal, which the host of a ceremonial gathering serves to their guests, before a tea ceremony.

Kamaboko

This is a kind of cured "surimi." Surimi is a processed seafood product, which is basically ground and combined with herbs and additives to create a seafood loaf. In this dish, the loaves are steamed, sliced and served chilled, with various dipping sauces. They can also be sliced and included in soup or noodle dishes.

Kenpi

This is a kind of snack food. It comprises of strips of candied sweet potato. They are similar to North American French fries or British chips, but are hard and sugary sweet in taste.

Kiritanpo

This is a kind of freshly cooked rice that is pounded until somewhat mashed. It is then formed into cylinders around Japanese cedar skewers and toasted over an open fire. This dish can be served either with sweet miso or used as dumplings in soups.

Miso Soup

This is a traditional soup, consisting of a stock called "dashi." Into this stock, softened miso paste is mixed. You can add many kinds of ingredients to miso soup, including vegetables, many varieties of seaweed or tofu. It is often served for breakfast.

Mochi

These are rice cakes made of "mochigome", which is a kind of short-grained Japanese rice. This rice is crushed and made into a fine paste. It is then molded into the desired shape. It is a traditional food for Japanese new year, but is also eaten year-round.

Motsunabe

A kind of "hot pot" dish, or "nabemono", in Japanese. Hot pot dishes involve having a central boiling pot, full of broth. The diners select from dishes of fresh ingredients and dip them in the pot, to cook them. This is the ultimate in fresh dining. The motsunabe variety is common in Japan. The central pot, in motsunabe, usually contains a variety of tripe or other guts from various animals. It is spiced with cabbage, garlic, chives and chili pepper or miso. Champon noodles are often included.

Natto

This is an acquired taste! Natto is a traditional dish, which is notorious for being hard to like. Even a lot of Japanese don't like natto. It is made from soybeans, which have been fermented with the bacteria "Bacillus Subtilis Var." It smells strongly, tastes even stronger and is very slimy. In Japan, it is most popular in the east.

Nikujaga

This is a dish made of meat, potato and onion. They're stewed in sweetened soya sauce and are mixed with vegetables and konnyaku (a kind of root vegetable). Thinly sliced beef is most common.

Ochazuke

A dish made by pouring green tea over cooked rice. Sometimes dashi or simply hot water is used. It is then topped with savory toppings, such as Japanese pickles, nori seaweed, sesame seeds, salted salmon, scallions or wasabi.

Oden

This is a common thing to eat in winter, in Japan. It is a soup, consisting of boiled eggs, daikon, konjac and fishcakes stewed in dashi broth. The exact ingredients vary, but "karashi" (a kind of mustard) is usually used as a condiment. This is a common food that is sold at Japanese food stalls.

Okonomiyaki

A kind of savory pancake, containing a variety of ingredient. In Japanese it means "what you like" and that illustrates the variety of okonomiyaki you might see. Common toppings and batters also vary, depending on the region, it is most commonly associated with Kansai and Hiroshima.

Omurice

This is a type of yoshoku (or western influenced cuisine). It is an omelet made of fried rice and topped with ketchup. It is, however, a popular dish, which is commonly cooked at home or at western style restaurants. It originated in Korea and was transmitted to Japan.

Onigiri

These are rice balls, made from white rice. They are usually formed into triangular or cylindrical shapes. They are often wrapped in nori seaweed, like sushi. Traditionally, onigiri is filled with pickled ume (a fruit), salted salmon, bonito flakes, tarako (salted roe), kombu seaweed or any other salty or sour ingredient.

Ramen

Well known in the west, ramen is a noodle soup dish. In Japan, it is usually served in a meat or fish broth, flavored with soya sauce or miso and topped with sliced pork, sea weed and green onions.

Sashimi

Raw or lightly cooked meat, sashimi requires very fresh ingredients. Sashimi can involve a variety of seafood, including fish, shrimp, octopus, squid or even such exotic creatures as sea urchin or whale meat. Sashimi is often the first course in formal Japanese meals and is considered the finest form of food, by many Japanese. It is often served with soya sauce dipping bowls, ginger and wasabi.

Sekihan

Meaning "red rice", it is rice boiled together with red beans. A traditional dish, the sticky variety of rice used bonds with the red adzuki beans, giving the dish its name.

Senbei

These are a kind of rice crackers. They can come in many shapes, sizes and flavors. They are usually savory, but can also be sweet. This food is often eaten with green tea or as a quick snack food. It is often offered to guests, in Japanese households.

Shabu-Shabu

A dish featuring thinly sliced beef, boiled in water. The name is derived from the sound made when stirring the pot. It consists, basically, of thinly sliced meat and vegetables, served with dipping sauces. This dish is similar to sukiyaki, in that in involves thin slices of meat and vegetables, but unlike sukiyaki, which is served all pre-assembled, the shabu-shabu diners cook each piece, themselves.

Shogayaki

This is a kind of Japanese ginger pork. It is grilled or fried and can also be made with beef. But pork is more common in Japan and it is the second most popular pork dish in Japan, after "tonkatsu".

Soba

This word means "buckwheat" in Japanese. And that's what soba is, a kind of buckwheat noodle. Soba noodles are thin and are served chilled or with a dipping sauce. They are also served in soups.

Sukiyaki

A kind of "hot pot" dish, or "nabemono", in Japanese. Hot pot dishes involve having a central boiling pot, full of broth. The diner's select from dishes of fresh ingredients and dip them in the pot, to cook them. This version of this dish consists of thin slices of beef, which are slowly cooked at the table, alongside vegetables and other ingredients, in a shallow iron pot, with a mixture of soya sauce, sugar and mirin in it.

The ingredients are dipped in a small bowl of raw, beaten eggs, after being cooked in the pot.

Sushi

The staple of the Japanophile's diet! Sushi is well-known and beloved, the world over. It generally involves a sticky kind of "sushi rice" mixed with other ingredients such as vegetables, seaweeds and raw or cooked fish. There are various kinds, including hosomaki, chumaki and futomaki, which are all rolled in a sheet of nori seaweed, with the seaweed layer on the outside. There is uramaki, which is reversed, with the nori layer on the inside and the rice layer on the outside. And then there is nigirizushi, which consists of a rectangular block of rice, with an ingredient placed on top of it. Oshizushi is a kind of rectangular sushi, where the ingredient is pressed into the rice, to make perfect geometric rectangles. Sushi is almost always served with soya dipping sauce, ginger and wasabi.

Taiyaki

This is a cake shaped like a fish and filled with red bean paste. It is sometimes filled with other ingredients, however, including custard, chocolate, cheese or pureed sweet potato.

Takoyaki

A ball-shaped snack made of wheat flour batter and cooked in a special pan. It is usually filled with pieces of octopus, pickled ginger, tempura scraps or green onion. The balls are brushed with takoyaki sauce (which is similar to worcestershire) and mayonnaise and is then sprinkled with bonito flakes.

Tempura

This is a kind of dish where seafood or vegetables are coated in a batter and deep-fried. Shrimp, shellfish or squid are common choices for tempura. The wheat and starch based batter is specialized and the method of doing a correct tempura is not easy.

Tonkatsu

A food consisting of a breaded, deep-fried pork cutlet. There are two varieties, loin and fillet. It is often served with shredded cabbage. It is often used as a sandwich filling or in combination with curry. This is the most popular pork dish in Japan.

Udon

A thick type of wheat flour noodle, udon is often served as a hot noodle soup. Such udon soup is usually flavoured with dashi, soya sauce and mirin. Such soup is usually topped with thinly cut scallions, tempura items or prawns. Shichimi is often added.

Umibudo

This is a kind of seaweed, often found around the Japanese island of Okinawa. It resembles mini strings of green pearls and pops in the mouth, like caviar. It should be soaked, before eaten and washed clean. But it is generally eaten raw and is very nutritious.

Unagi

This is the Japanese word for "eel" and that's what this dish consists of. It is a common ingredient in Japanese cooking and can be a part of many dishes. However, it is listed separately because eel is a special food, in Japan. There are entire restaurants, devoted to unagi and grilled unagi, on a stick, is common fare in street vendor's stalls.

Wakame Salad

A salad made from the sea vegetable, wakame. It is usually mixed with tofu and salad vegetables, like cucumber, and dressed with soya sauce and rice vinegar.

 The Japanophile's Handbook

Yakiniku

This basically means "grilled meat" and is the Japanese version of barbecue. In fact, this is an adopted food, borrowed from the west. But the Japanese style is a bit different. It commonly refers to a style of cooking bite-sized meat, primarily beef, and vegetables on a griddle, over flames of wood charcoals, or a gas or electric grill.

Yakisoba

This is a fried noodle dish. In spite of the name, it doesn't use soba (buckwheat noodles). It is cooked with thin wheat flour noodles, a mixture of fried meats and vegetables, and eaten with oyster sauce.

Yakitori

Yakitori is grilled chicken, skewered on steel or bamboo skewers. They are grilled on a charcoal fire and seasoned with either tare sauce (a sweet sauce) or salt. This is another kind of street vendor food, that exists everywhere, selling yakitori, exclusively.

Yakizakana

This is a kind of grilled fish. A herring is dried, very quickly, with salt added as a preservative, and its own eggs inside it. It becomes semi-dry and soft and juicy, after being lightly grilled.

Yuba

This food is made from soybeans. During the boiling of soy milk, a film of skin forms on the liquid surface. These films are collected and dried into yellow sheets, called tofu skin. Because tofu is more processed than yuba, it has a slightly different flavour than tofu.

Yudofu

This is basically, cubes of tofu, placed in a bowl of hot water, and topped with grated daikon, scallions and soya sauce. It is one of Japan's signature delicate, minimalist and delicious dishes.

Zoni

Zoni is a soup containing mochi rice cakes. The dish is strongly associated with the Japanese New Year. It is considered one of the most auspicious dishes, which is traditional eaten during new year.

5.4 The Japanese People

If you are a genuine, card-carrying Otaku, then you probably have some secret desire to communicate with Japanese people, at some point, travel to Japan, or maybe even participate in the culture. Of course, we can relate to these lofty dreams, being Japanophiles ourselves. But the true blue Otaku needs to learn, at the very least, a few basic facts about the Japanese national temperament, and what major faux pas to avoid, if you want to interact with the culture, appropriately, and not in the way a Weeaboo might. You need to avoid the temptation to act shamelessly, ignorantly, and in all other ways like a Weeaboo, by learning a few things about the culture.

This is not a book on the definition of the Japanese culture, so we will not provide you with a comprehensive appraisal of the culture. The curious Otakus can study those things for themselves, by reading one of the many high quality books on the subject. We will, however, explain the most central problem, which Weeaboos encounter, when first trying to ineptly relate to the Japanese people. That being, the Japanese temperament is not at all like the American or even the western temperament. Whereas, in the west, individuality and drive are considered positive qualities, they are not seen the same way, in Japan. In that country, if you are too much of a rugged individualist, it might actually indicate that you are a weak, unreliable character and that you are selfish, in a childish, willful

kind of way.

It is hard to explain, to westerners, but it can be summed up in the following examples. In the west, for the most part, everyone is competing with each other. And so, if you are assertive and individualistic, you are admired, because you are a contender in the arena of life. Although there is much kindness in the west, regardless, considerate and empathetic people are often considered weak and ill-equipped to deal with life, because the society is, of course, modelled on the idea of competition and confrontation. Not everyone is the same, of course, in the west, and there are certainly a lot of empathetic, kind people, in the west, but, for the most part, it can be said that western culture is individualistic and competitive. In such a culture, it is sometimes a losing battle, trying to be considerate, because you are often repaid by aggressors taking advantage or sheisters trying to exploit you. But, imagine for a minute that society was full of considerate people? And that it was the exact opposite — meaning that you were expected to be considerate, because everyone else is? In such a society, it would only work if everyone was equally considerate. Well, that is no fantasy; that is what Japanese society is actually like. It is a massive population, which is only polite and held together because people are, for the most part, considerate to each other. Think of all the people packed into such a small island and yet still it manages to have one of the lowest crime rates in the world. It is because of this national temperament that favors consideration for others. Now, knowing this, you can see why people who are too pushy, willful or confrontational are seen as selfish and weak. They are the weak links in this endless chain of empathetic and considerate citizens and they threaten to unravel it all. There are, of course, independent and creative people and individual expression happening in Japan, but tempered with a sense of duty.

For this reason, the number one virtue in Japan is not assertiveness, it is empathy. If you are assertive, you will not be seen as strong. You will be seen as too weak-minded to keep it together and join in the general culture of consideration, empathy and duty to your society. You will impress a Japanese person if you can resist the urge to be selfish and put someone else's feelings and interests ahead of

your own. This is why Japanese service providers do not accept tips, at stores and restaurants, because they are serving you out of a sense of duty and a genuine empathy for your situation and your needs. It is almost an affront to their national temperament of empathy, to imply they were doing it for something as crass as money.

What is more, it is essential to understand the different way in which Japanese people make friends. If you're American, for example, and you're relatively outgoing, you might strike up a conversation with someone, in a cafeteria line or something, you might "click", find you're compatible, and before the end of the day, you're best buddies. It won't happen that way in Japan. Japanese friendships take time. Because the Japanese do not believe in outwardly expressing their emotions, except to their most intimate friends (and even then, not like in the west), you often will not even know they consider you a good friend until a year or more has passed. It takes considerable time for them to see you as a friend and it is something you have to earn, from real effort and plenty of demonstrations of persistent loyalty. Now, this may seem cold, or distant, from a western perspective, but there is good reason for this. The Japanese have two words: "uchi" meaning inside and "soto" meaning outside. Uchi refers to their close friends, the people in their inner circle. Soto refers to anyone who is outside that circle. And how they relate and communicate to the two are drastically different. To the soto, they are still polite and they might be outgoing, on the surface, but they will keep them far away, until they are considered considerate and trustworthy enough to slip their way into the uchi category. Once you are uchi, the Japanese version of friendship is entire universes beyond the average American friendship! Uchi friends are for life. Uchi friends represent a sacred duty. A Japanese friend, who has become an uchi friend, is the one who will come to your aid, in your time of need, when all your western "friends" have turned their back and walked away. So, the true blue uchi friendship of a Japanese person is an incredibly rewarding thing to gain. But like anything which is of true value, it takes a lot to earn it. Be patient, understand that true expressions of friendship will take time, show self-discipline, remain loyal, remain patient, and you're sure to gain a true blue uchi friend before long.

If you can fully understand the fundamental difference, between Japanese temperament and the western ones, then you can avoid 90% of the mistakes that Weeaboos make, when trying to relate to the Japanese. In the spirit of empathy, however, we'll help you even more, by providing a few helpful tips that might help you avoid any additional misunderstandings, if ever you encounter a genuine Japanese person. We will list here, a few of the biggest faux pas, which foreigners commonly commit.

COMMON FAUX PAS COMMITED BY WESTERNERS

Failing to remove footware when entering a home.

Treating someone's business card casually. In Japan, business cards need to be treated with great reverence.

Tipping service providers.

Talking on the phone in the company of others. That includes on trains or in restaurants.

Showing tattoos in public. Unless you're in harajuku or something, tattoo are associated with gangsters.

Disrespecting food. Wasting food is frowned upon. The Japanese also give thanks before and after eating.

Nervous leg-shaking is particularly abhorent.

Blowing your nose in public.

Playing with chopsticks. Never stab a stick into your food vertically, pass food with them or place them directly on the table. Never share chopsticks.

Aggressive or even assertive behavior. Any kind of threatening action is considered very crude and rude.

Eating of smoking, while walking, is bad.

Silence is always preferable over bluster.

As a side note, you should always be aware of what is happening around you, when in Japan. Watch people's faces, because people will not always tell you if you make a jerk of yourself. This is because they are too considerate to make you "lose face."

5.5 Popular Culture in Japan

If you want to fully understand the culture we all love, you need to know about it, in its entirety. Life in Japan, nowadays, is nothing like a Kurosawa movie, and only the contemptible Weeaboo thinks that it is. In order to be a whole, well-rounded Otaku, you need to be up on Japanese popular culture, as much as you may be up on anime, samurai philosophy or the canon of Square Enix games.

Japan's culture is thriving and always on the move — always evolving. We can't possibly express it all here and you're encouraged to explore the endless publications and websites, which cover Japanese popular culture, in order to become suitably knowledgeable about it. But we can, at least, summarize the main areas of the culture and point you to the publications and websites where you are most likely to find good information. We've already covered a lot of areas of the culture, in this book, such as the films, the anime, the manga and the video games. But, to help you attain a well-rounded knowledge, we'll now sum up the remaining significant points of the popular culture, based on our experience and research.

5.5.1 J-pop

Referred to as J-pop, Japanese popular music is a thriving industry. The modern incarnation of J-pop emerged in the 1990s and encapsulates a variety of musical styles, including pop, rock, rap, dance and soul. It has produced innumerable musicians, musical groups and pop idols. It all started in Japan, which has been the leader in popular music, in Asia, since the 1920s. The Korean K-pop movement and other popular movements, on the continent, followed the J-pop lead. There are many musicians, famous in Japan, who every Japanophile should know about, and we will list them, individually, in the following history. But first, we should explain the fundamentals of how Japanese pop idols work and give some examples of idols.

J-pop is a complex component of the culture and needs to be explained, first, in order to be fully understood by western readers. The pop idol culture has become big, in Japan, and is similar, in a way, to the western pop idol craze, that's been happening since Elvis Presley and the Beatles. Although, the Japanese pop idols are possibly even more of an influence on youth culture, than these famous idols were. Unlike the western pop stars, the Japanese idols are considered role models for the youth, and are expected to be genuine positive examples for young girls and youths to follow. Young idols are chosen, from a very early age, and groomed for a career as a successful J-pop idol. The screening for children, who dream of propelling to pop idol success are rigorous and you can be sure that any pop idol you see has likely done a massive amount to earn that career. So legendary is this process of "creating pop idols" in Japan, there is an entire genre of manga, devoted to it. Idol manga chronicles the rise of an idol from obscurity to great fame.

A perfect modern example of this process is the group Babymetal, which exploded into fame, both in Japan and the west, with their 2014 break out, self-titled, album. The lead singer, Suzuka Nakamoto (aka Su-Metal), was signed to a talent agency, before she was 10 years old, and was used in the kid's idol group "Karen Girl's" and then in the young teen band "Sakura Gakiun", by the time she was an adolescent. With high school graduation, she was chosen as the lead singer for Babymetal, which is geared more to adults. The unique fusion of young girls playing heavy metal, combined with the heavy references to traditional Japanese culture has proven very popular, and besides creating an entirely new genre has also accumulated many Japanophile fans. I admit that I can't watch the video for their hit song "Megitsune" without have a bit of an Otaku nerdgasm. It is recommended curious Otaku, who want a taste of modern J-pop start with this song. The fact "megitsune" is a female form of Kitsune fox (the magical fox spirits which serve the Shinto god Inari) mixed with the endless traditional cultural references (including the traditional Kitsune mask, used for ceremonies and traditional theater) along with the extra boon of giving you a taste of a modern J-pop idol make this song a true Otaku educational tool.

Sakura's career follows the standard trajectory of a modern pop idol, in Japan. However, not every idol follows this path. Some of them, such as the currently uber-popular pop singer Kyary Pamyu Pamyu started as a fashion blogger and an avant-garde fashion artist, in Tokyo's legendary fashion district, Harajuku. Kiriko Takemura, which is her real name, gained some popularity as a fashion blogger first and then was noticed for her highly creative and unusual fashion sense, while walking in the Harajuku district. This district is famous for being a place where creative fashion artists, like Kiriko, go to be seen and showcase their fashion sense. Eventually, she became so well-noticed and gained enough of a following that she was approached by organizers of fashion shows and media events, to participate in the shows. There, her fame caught the attention of the producer of her favorite musical group, Perfume. He suggested she try out as a singer, and so the legend was born.

So, there are a few ways to become a pop idol, in Japan. I like to follow the popular fashion bloggers and determine which ones I think are likely to succeed, the way Kiriko Takemura, did. Like a lot of true Japanophiles, I have my chosen Japanese model, who I am dedicated to and admire for her unique characteristics and creativity. For me, it is Yuri Nakagawa, who started as a fashion blogger, just like Kiriko, and has since become popular as a model and the host or DJ of fashion and promotional events. She is currently an official blogger for JFW fashion, which is an international fashion exhibition, organized by the famous Japanese fashion newspaper and magazine, Senken Shimbun. It's been such a pleasure to see her career take the same course as other famous Japanese celebrities, and I recommend any dedicated Otaku attach themselves to a chosen model, in this way, in order to get the full Japanophile experience. I liked Yuri so much that I included her in my novel, "Trueman Bradley - The Next Great Detective." In the novel, the protagonist, who is a private detective and also an Otaku, obsessed with manga, is also obsessed with Yuri Nakagawa. He uses her Instagram posts as a source of inspiration to help him uncover the secret of resonance, the lost art of instinctual inference, which he purports was a secret tactic of Sherlock Holmes.

If you are ever in Japan, you must visit Harajuku, given that it is the

incubator for so much of Japan's avant garde creativity, including future J-pop idols and musicians. Artists, fashion models and innovative creatives, of all kinds, are on display, in the district. Any true lover of the culture should be able to spend weeks in the district and never get bored. So vast and varied is the Japanese creative scene that we can't possibly express it here, but we'll point you to a few of the best websites you can visit, regularly, in order to keep up to date on the Japanese arts and pop scene.

www.tokyohive.com - Most popular English J-pop news service.
www.aramajapan - Entertainment news focusing on J-pop and film.
www.japanesestreets.com - Harajuku and street fashion.

5.5.2 History of J-pop

Japanese popular music began in the early 1920s. Taking their cues from the jazz age, which was emerging in America, at the time, Japanese jazz first sprouted in the fertile entertainment districts of Osaka and Kobe. This marked the beginning of Japan's popular music, which was much different from all forms of traditional music, which had existed before. Although Japan adopted the new music, enthusiastically, traditionalists banned the swing dance clubs that popped up, as a result. Just like in the west, the conservatives considered this music decadent and a corrupting influence on youth. As a result, several jazz artists of the day, including Ryoichi Hattori and Koiichi Sugii, tried to lessen the threatening nature of this foreign sound by blending it with traditional forms of Japanese music and using distinctively Japanese themes for his new songs. This established a tradition of mixing new music with older Japanese traditions, which still exists, in modern J-pop music. Although under a different name, this popular music movement was, in fact, the beginnings of J-pop. In spite of the best efforts of the traditionalists, the jazz and country music scene grew so quickly that 1952 was proclaimed the "Year of the Jazz Boom" in Japan.

In 1956, Japan entered the rock-and-roll scene, beginning with a group named Kozaka Kazuya and the Wagon Masters, who emulated the style of Elvis Presley. One of the most famous examples of a rock-and-roll song mingled with traditional Japanese

music, from this era, was "Let's Look Up and Walk" by Sakamoto Kyū. During this era, as well, a lot of cover bands popped up, creating Japanese covers of popular western songs. It's thought this period of western covers is where karaoke originated from, which the Japanese invented and has since spread all over the world.

After traditional rock-and-roll declined, in the early 1970s, Japanese music began to evolve beyond the simple singer with a guitar format, which had dominated its music scene, and became more complex. It also began to become more independent of the west and entirely original music forms began to emerge. The period of covers was over and an artistic shift, called "New Music", emerged. This is considered, by some, to be the actual beginning of "J-pop" because this was the time when Japanese popular music began to forge its own identity, independent of the west, and when the subject matter of music became more "pop" in content. Subjects like love and personal issues now became the norm, just like with western pop music.

Groups like Happy End were formative influences, during this period, combining rock music with traditional Japanese music. Unlike previous cover bands, they sang in Japanese and created their own hits. They became so popular, in Asia, they were dubbed the "Japanese Beatles." An internationally renowned musician, Isao Tomita, released an album in 1972 called "Electric Samurai" which was the first Japanese album to use electronic synthesizer music — a phenomenon which was avant garde at the time, even in the west. Electronic music — still popular in Japan — really took off and helped forge J-pop's unique identity. The student of early J-pop might want to listen to such influential albums as "Ice World" (1973), by Inuoe Yousui and "Benzaiten" (1974), by Osamu Kitajima.

Although pioneering musical groups, like this, helped to keep the discotheques running, in Japan and Asia, during the 1970s, nothing became a runaway hit, internationally. It was not until the late 70s and early 80s, when Eikichi Yazawa tried to become an international sensation, that Japanese music first became more widely known in the west. He released "Time, Stop" (1978), which sold over 639,000

copies, and other albums such as "It's Just Rock and Roll" and "Flash in Japan." Yazawa's music was wildly popular in Japan. Although they became known in the west, they were not commercially successful there. During the same time, the pivotal band, the "Yellow Magic Orchestra", began experimenting with a more elaborate form of electronic music, similar to early techno. Becoming incredibly popular in Japan, they really helped to cement the still popular Japanese genre of technopop. Their legendary album, "Solid State Survivor" (1980), broke through all previous records for a Japanese album by selling over two million copies, worldwide. It was so extremely influential in Japanese music that its listeners were called the "YMO Generation" and this generation was profoundly influenced, musically, by this pioneering musical group.

In the 1980s J-pop really took off, alongside the rise of major pop idols in the west. The amount of influential and original bands increased, during this time. Some of the most important musical groups to emerge in the 80s were RC Succession, Blue Hearts, Anzen Chitai, Southern All-Stars and The Checkers. Most of these groups, by and large, were influenced by previous generations of Japanese pop musicians, but a few were influenced by the so-called "New Romanticism" of 80s music, which is typified by such groups and Duran Duran. Bands like Boøwy and TM Network are a few examples. Boøwy, in particular, is considered another major pioneer in the ever-evolving pop scene of Japan and influenced many future generations of musicians.

The late 80s were an important time, for J-pop, because many important genres, in the history of the movement, were created during these years. At this time, the first Japanese "girl group" was born. Called Princess Princess, this group was like the grandmother of all the ubiquitous girl bands that are now all over Japan. This is the band that gave birth to them all. In 1989, their hit singles "Diamonds" and "World's Hottest Summer" held both first and second place in the Oricon music charts — which should give some indication of their massive popularity, at the time. In addition, the 80s, in general, spawned a genre of Japanese music called "City Pop", which was a type of music that celebrated or commented on the setting of Japan's now massive and cosmopolitan metropolises.

It's thought the growth of car stereos, in Japan, gave birth to this genre. A great majority of these City Pop albums were written about Tokyo. One great example of this genre is the album "Reflections" (1981) by Akira Terao. This style of music continued to be popular, until the early 1990s and really reached its peak in the late 80s.

Also in the late 80s, Japan's version of "hair bands" emerged. In the style of bands like KISS and other androgynous, heavy metal or glamour-based bands of the era, the Japanese called this genre "Visual Kei" because of their emphasis on visual presentation. Some of the names to remember, in order to be educated about the origins of this genre are such musical trail-blazers as X Japan and Buck-tick. X Japan was particularly popular and were the first Japanese musical group to really break out into the west. Legendary X Japan albums, like "Blue Blood" (1989) and "Jealousy" (1991), were released through American record labels and enjoyed genuine popular and commercial success, around the world. Even today, X Japan still enjoys great popularity, among certain groups, and has an enduring fan base. By being the first real "break out" group, X Japan created the new and somewhat separate phenomenon of J-rock, which is always growing and evolving, alongside J-pop. J-rock is still sometimes called Visual Kei and that shows the influence that the late 80s and such groups as X Japan had on Japanese music.

Coming into the 1990s, J-pop began to assume its current form. Not only was the term J-pop invented (by a radio station) during this decade, but the current commercial nature of the industry also came into being. Realizing Japanese music was now a prized product, capable of making money all over the world, Japanese music companies started taking control of the industry. Most prominent of these music companies was the "Being Agency." This company churned out so many of the popular musical groups of the 90s that it was often referred to as the "Being System" — given the entire industry often seemed to be a part of that company's master plan. Because the newly invented term of J-pop covered all possible forms of popular music, from rap to alternative grunge, these popular 90s groups formed a diverse spectrum of styles. Some of the most famous and successful groups were B'z (rock duo), Deen (pop), T-Bolan (rock), B.B. Queens (pop), Field of View (rock),

Zard (pop), Wands (rock) and Maki Ohguro (early female pop idol). Japanese hip-hop was also developing during this period, with such early groups as Buddha Brand and Scha Dara Parr. Unlike western hip-hop, the early Japanese versions lacked a lot of the machismo and often tackled social questions. Scha Dara Parr has been compared, in style and treatment, to the Beastie Boys. But it was legendary hip-hop artist, Zeebra, who really brought the genre into the mainstream, with his popular single "Mr. Dynamite" (1999). Some of these artists, such as B'z and Zard, sold albums in the tens of millions and are still considered some of the best-selling musical groups in Japanese history, or even overall world history. So, clearly, Japan's attempt to cash in on its J-pop industry was a huge success.

Dance and techno, during the 90s, continued to grow, with such artists as Globe, Hitomi, Ami Suzuki, TRF, Yuki Uchida and Tomomi Kahala, dominating the scene. The popularity of J-rock and Visual Kei enjoyed a resurgence in the late 90s, with such extremely popular groups as Glay, Luna Sea and L'Arc-en-Ciel coming onto the scene. A lot of these "new wave" J-rock bands are still around and still massively popular. Following the wave of western boy bands, in the 1990s, Japan also produced a prolific output of boy bands. Created by J-pop producer, "Johnny & Associates", some of the most popular bands were SMAP, Arashi, KinKi Kids and V6. Girl bands also rose up, at the same time, with groups like Speed and Morning Musume becoming very popular.

In the early 2000s, uber-popular pop idols began to become a real thing. This period marked the real birth of Japan's pop idol phenomenon. Idols of the early 00s, like Hikaru Utada, broke all previous records. Her most famous album, "First Love" (1999) enjoyed so much popularity, through the early 00s, that it has since become the best selling album in Japanese history. This time was dominated by female pop idols, like Utada, who played all their own music and wrote all their own songs. The tradition of thoughtful and talented female leads, created during this time, is still dominant in modern-day J-pop and left a lasting impression on the culture. Besides Utada, some of the biggest pop idols of the period were women like Mai Kuraki, Ringo Shiina, Ayumi Hamasaki and Misia.

During this time, too, hip-hop and R&B started to assert itself, outside of the fringes and into the mainstream of J-pop. Popular rock bands, like Orange Range, began to incorporate hip-hop into their sound and new R&B acts, like Chemistry, Halcali (female artist) and Ken Hirai were, occasionally, dominating the Oricon music charts. The fact that Chemistry's album "The Way We Are" (2001) sold over 1.14 million copies in the first week and debuted at #1 on the charts shows how popular these genres were, in the 00s.

Coming into the 10s, J-pop has exploded to such proportions that it is almost impossible to list them all or to properly educate the eager Japanophile on all the different genres and sub-genres that have popped up, in recent years. It's been calculated that musical groups in Japan have jumped up 500%, from the 00s to the 10s. So, I'm not kidding when I say it is practically an impossible task to describe J-pop, beyond the 00s, in one short chapter. In order to educate you Otakus about this, I'd need to write an entire book on the topic. But I will mention some of the most popular pop idols, at present, so that you can feel properly informed — as all self-respecting Otaku should — about what's happening in J-pop, these days. Idol groups are the biggest movement of the 10s, so far. The most popular groups being Babymetal, AKB48, Momoiro Clover Z, Kanjani Eight, Fairies, Arashi and the venerable Morning Musume, which constantly renews its ranks with younger artists. Idols continue to go strong, as well, as an essential part of J-pop. One of the biggest developments being the rise of Kyary Pamyu Pamyu and her Harajuku influenced performance style. This movement promises to draw a lot of new talent from the "grass roots" of Japan's artistic communities and make more "YouTube-like" pop stars, who derive their fan bases from followers and subscribers, rather than record labels. This is the way the entire society is going and J-pop is no exception. This is why I recommend watching popular artists, like Harajuku models, and guessing which ones appear to be on the rise.

As a final point, I have to mention two things. One is the phenomenal rise of the so-called "Vocaloids" which are a form of computer-generated pop idol. This is another example of an entirely Japan-invented genre. The term vocaloid actually refers to a type of

musical software, developed by the Japanese company Yamaha in 2004. This software allowed users to easily create studio-quality musical compositions using entirely software-created sources. It would have simply been just another piece of musical software, had it not been for the release of the "Hatsune Miku Vocaloid" software set, in 2007, which paired the song-creating technology with a cute, anime-inspired mascot named Hatsune Miku. Since then, Miku has become a sensation. An all-new phenomenon — a famous pop idol who doesn't actually exist. Amazing as it may seem, Miku has become a part of the general scene of J-pop. Since then, many other famous "Vocaloids" have emerged, including Megurine Luka, Kaito, Gumi, Kagamine Len, Kagamine Rin, Iroha Nekomura, VY2, Oliver, Meiko, SeeU, Miriam, IA and the Kagamine Twins. If you want to get an idea about popular vocaloid music, you can begin with some of Hatsune Miku's most popular: "VOiCE" (2010), "BadBye" (2011) and "Last Night, Good Night" (2008).

Secondly, it is important for all Otaku to realize the amount of J-pop music to be found in anime. If any, among you, wonder why I go into such detail, concerning the history of J-pop, it is because, for one things, all Japanophiles should be naturally interested in this topic. But even more importantly, for those large percentage of you who came by your Japanophilia through anime, you aren't getting the full experience unless you realize the significance of the band creating your favorite theme song, or at least have a passing knowledge of the scene. For example, the first season theme song of the anime series Bleach ("Asterisk" by Orange Range) has a full version that only adds to the no-holds-barred geek-out experience of fandom, when it is explored, discovered and listened to. Extending our fandom sensibilities to the bands, themselves, help us to strengthen our fandom and even expand it into new, related areas, which make our Otaku experience richer and more satisfying.

As a way of helping my brethren explore these rich veins of fandom glory, I encourage you to expand on your knowledge, by looking into the bands who created your favorite anime song and educating yourself into how they fit into J-pop, using this chapter as a guide.

6.1 Japanese Spirituality

The Otaku life is not a part time occupation. It's an all-encompassing passion. This is not the territory of the half-assed, by any means. No, the committed Japanophile should see it as an almost religious calling, if not a completely religious one. And to that end, all true Otaku should be aware of the spiritual and philosophical traditions of Japan, and take those to heart, or even adopt them, if possible. At least, in an oblique, western Otaku kind of way. Don't stride into Kyoto's Ryōan-ji temple and declare yourself the most dedicated Zen Buddhist monk since Dōgen. As in all other things, the true Otaku should always keep a respectful distance away from the real and actual Japanese religious institutions, lest you accidentally transform into a Weeaboo, who is trying too hard to please and is desperately starving for acceptance. No, the real-deal Otakus, amongst us, should they be interested in these religions, should create their own, western Otaku, versions of these spiritual practices — which they can then proceed to diligently practice, if they so desire, with their community of like-minded Japanophiles.

So the fifth commandment is something which most of you already have, concerning all things Japanese: complete obsession! More specifically, you should practice the Japanese spiritual path, in some way or form. You don't have to become a Buddhist, but you should at least know what Shinto is and appreciate it, viscerally. You should be so into the culture, that it's a daily, obsessive spiritual path, for you. That is the fifth commandment of the true Japanophile. You must adopt at least some element of the religious or philosophical outlook of the country and its people. This can be anything from the obsessive study of Zen koans, to the purchase of a Shinto Torii gate to the adoption of the full Bushido code. So long as it is Japanese, is a major aspect of the culture, and is agreeable to you, there is really no area of the spiritual outlook you cannot adopt as your own, in order to fulfill the fifth commandment.

Those who wish to focus on the rich heritage of samurai philosophy, in order to fulfill this particular requirement of Otaku life, may wish to acquire a copy of our other book, "Instruction Manual for the 21st Century Samurai," in order to get a concise picture of what it means to truly live the life of the traditional samurai, in this day and age. I, myself, follow the teachings of my own samurai manual, in combination with a general Zen Buddhist outlook and a powerful liking for the Shinto deity, Inari Ōkami.

Being the Kami (Shinto god) of foxes, among other things, Inari is the patron deity of the magical and formidable Kitsune foxes, of legend and anime lore. Inari brings success, fruitfulness and is the patron deity of the samurai sword — that all important symbol of all that is right with the world, in the eyes of the Japanophile. And so, it is a fitting god for any admirer of the samurai ethic or lover of Japan's cultural heritage. In fact, one or two Shinto rites to Inari Ōkami is the spiritual path I most recommend for any Otaku or Japanophile, who is wishing to fulfill their fifth commandment requirements. As, Inari is not only the deity which is, perhaps, the most "Japanese" of all Kami, but is also closely entwined both with anime and video game culture. Given that, Inari's primary messengers (the Kitsune foxes) having been depicted or prominently featured in many manga, anime and video games,

including other major areas of Japanese culture — from Babymetal to traditional Japanese samurai philosophy. Making Inari Ōkami, in the eyes of this author anyways, the most appropriate patron Kami of Japanophiles and western Otakus, the world over.

However, recommendations aside, this will always be a personal choice. And in the interest of helping each Japanophile to decide for themselves, which philosophy most suits their temperament, we will now outline the basic philosophies and spiritual practices, that most express the Japanese outlook.

6.2 Shinto

The most "Japanese" of religions, this is the indigenous religion of Japan and, therefore, from a Japanophile perspective, the most important one. Shinto is often referred to as "animism" in the west, meaning it is a religion which doesn't focus on a single creator deity, but rather believes that many things, people and places can have their own spiritual energy. But Shinto is so much more than that and these western labels express, to a large degree, how little the west understands complicated religions like Shinto. It is not as simple as following an ethical formula and then going to heaven. Just like daily life, itself, Shinto is complicated and multi-faceted. In that way, it is a much more realistic and practical religion than those in the west. It may be hard for westerners to grasp, intuitively, but we will try to outline the main points of the religion, here.

Shinto means, literally, "Way of the Gods" and centers around divine spirits called "Kami." Although this word corresponds, roughly, to the English word "gods", it is actually a much more profound idea than you'd expect from a western god, like Zeus or Freya. In Shinto, there are a few actual gods, with names, like Inari or Amaterasu (who is the Kami that created Japan), but, in truth, anything that gives off a sacred essence is a Kami, to some degree. A divine concept, like justice, would have its own powerful Kami, because this word has a positive essence and significance; a beautiful natural scene, which inspires wonder and pure, beautiful thoughts in the viewer also has Kami-power and has its own Kami. Because the

Japanese language often doesn't specify singular or plural subjects, the word Kami can also be used to refer to spiritual energy. So, if you say something has Kami, it means it has great spiritual energy.

Learning all this, you can see how the western explorers, coming over with their simple morality tales, were overwhelmed by the vast concept that is Shinto. It is not a simple religion or a religion for the simple. In Shinto, anyone can have Kami, and therefore be a little bit of a Kami god. You may not be Amaterasu, but you can, at least, reach the lower rungs of the Kami scale. And by petitioning the higher Kami, in solemn ceremonies, you may reach even higher than that. In order to have Kami, something needs to have "purity." This idea of "purity" and "impurity" is a very important concept in Shinto and basically replaces the western religious concepts of good and evil. In Shinto, if you perform an impure act, you lose Kami, are spiritually weaker, and ill fortune, universal shunning and karmic punishments will be yours. Whereas, if you are pure in your dealings and inspire a positive feeling of love or respect in others, you accumulate Kami and good fortune naturally comes your way, as people are positively swayed by your good energies and the more powerful Kami, above you, begin to take notice of your energies.

In nature, you can sense Kami by how much a given location inspires awe and reverence, in you. If you come across a stunning natural vista, odds are you are experiencing powerful Kami. This place, in all likelihood, is full of Kami, and that is why you are awed. And, what is more, it probably has materialized for itself a semi-material Kami god, who can then be petitioned and prayed to by those who may wish to gain the Kami's favor and good wishes. The Kami accumulated by deceased relatives or revered historical heroes can also come into your life and bless you if you perform similar rites and prayers, in the name of these revered individuals. Having learned all this, you can see how fascinating and complex Shinto is and how many infinite combinations of Kami power can come together to form, literally, millions of Kami. The Shinto universe is, therefore, infinite in its scope. There is a hint of that Japanese view of the infinite nature of Kami power in the phrase "Yaoyorozu no

Kami", which literally means "The Eight Million Kami" which refers to the sum total of Kami power, existent in the universe. Although referencing the figure eight million, it is closer to the truth that Kami power is seen as being veritably infinite, at its source.

If you want to become Shinto, you will probably need to do so on your own because there is no actual "Shinto church" as there is in Christianity or other western religions. People tend to practice it regionally or in private sects, which would be almost impossible for a westerner to penetrate. Creating or joining groups of like-minded westerners might be your best bet, and you can join our group at www.samuraicollective.com, which is intended for those who admire all Japanese spiritualism, including Shinto, Zen Buddhism and the traditional samurai philosophies, adapted to western sensibilities. Gathering together with other western Japanophiles who wish to explore these philosophies is your best bet for finding support, along your spiritual path. It is highly recommended, however, to all Japanophiles, even if you aren't interested in becoming Shinto, that you read up on Shinto and come to know the basic philosophies, as it really is an essential ingredient in the true Otaku life. Shinto is highly referenced in all forms of Japanese culture and so it is essential that we understand the references.

6.3 Zen

The second most significant religion, in Japan, is Zen Buddhism. Being the official religion of most samurai, throughout the country's history, it has exerted a massive influence on the culture, second only to Shinto. It's done much to form the national character, which is more stoic and philosophical than many other nations. Zen monasteries, such as Ryōan-ji in Kyoto, are legendary sites of spiritual pilgrimage and Buddhist rituals and festivals are closely entwined with the daily life of Japanese. Often, Buddhism will blend with Shinto and Buddhist sutras will be offered up for prayer at the same time as Shinto blessings. The two religions have fused, to a large extent, and so it is just as important for all true Otaku to understand Zen, at least on a basic level, as it is for them to understand Shinto. Zen is notoriously difficult to understand and

monks spend their whole lives trying to learn the spiritual lessons. So, of course, we won't be giving a complete lesson on this deeply profound and philosophical religion. However, as we did with Shinto, we will try to explain the main points, here, so that all interested Japanophiles can more easily study Zen on their own.

Like all forms of Buddhism, Zen originated in India. However, unlike all other varieties of the religion, Zen is thought to be the original spiritual practice passed down from Buddha, himself. It is the "day-to-day" form of spiritual discipline, which the Buddha himself practiced. Disciples of Buddha learned this pure and undiluted form of practice from the Buddha, where it was later transported to China (called Chan Buddhism). Later, in the 12th century, it was brought to Japan, where it was renamed Zen Buddhism and made a lasting impact.

In the Zen view, the other denominations of Buddhism became too elaborate — relying heavily on magic sutras, deity worship and rote memorization of endless books on Buddhist theory. These needless embellishments distract from the simple message of enlightened living, which Zen practitioners believe was Buddha's core message. Although Zen does involve the usual sitting meditation, reciting sutras and the reading of the Buddhist classical canon, these things are considered mere learning aids and are seen as far more secondary then they are in other forms of Buddhism. In Zen, the all-important core purposes are the same as they were for the Buddha. That is, learning to live each moment in mindfulness, awareness and with an enlightened perspective about reality.

Zen Buddhism became popular in Japan for several significant reasons. Firstly, the mystical simplicity of the religion, lacking all the elaborate add-ons of the other denominations, matches the Japanese esthetic of shibumi, which manifests itself in those things which are simple, graceful and minimalistic. The central message of Zen is to learn to drop all the unimportant extra baggage that comes from existence on this Earth and learning to identify the few, profound concepts that are actually important. The religion defines itself through its sublime simplification of life. Even the temples

themselves, with their Spartan meditation halls and modest, yet captivating, rock gardens, fit in perfectly with the shibumi tastes of the Japanese national temperament. Whether these strictly physical features were always inherent to Zen or were a result of Japan's influence on Zen, the fact remains that the aesthetic Zen monastery became an essential mainstay of the culture, which endures today.

Secondly, and more importantly, the practice of Zen, which teaches a person to accept suffering and reduce their attachment to worldly things, appealed greatly to the samurai classes, who often faced the possibility of death in battle. In feudal Japan, where a warrior might not live through his next sword duel, it was incredibly helpful to be versed in a religion that allowed you to be braver in the face of death and more willing to risk leaving this Earth, given they had less attachments to what they would leave behind. Unlike other religions, which may promise paradise or try to circumvent fear of death in such roundabout ways, Zen actually taught the mind to accept misfortune, pain and death, by the profound teachings of the masters, which helped the samurai see how worldly things were not actually important, when the true enlightened perspective was learned. This religion didn't merely state that worldly things weren't important, they actually showed their adherents why it wasn't important through the profound experience of enlightenment. It is hard to explain the deep insights of enlightenment, but Zen could lead the student down that road to understanding this profound truth. Enlightenment is not an intellectual concept, but a deep, visceral understanding of something very profound. So, Zen offered more to them than any other religion. Through it, the samurai could literally lose all fear, without having to pretend. They literally did risk death with a light heart. Or rather, with an enlightened heart; having truly gleaned the spiritual insight that made life clear to them.

Zen enlightenment is notoriously hard to attain and even harder to explain. In my lifelong study of it, I have come to gain some understanding of what enlightenment feels like and how it enlarges your perspective and simplifies your priorities, but even with all these insights I have difficulty explaining it. To experience it yourself, it is recommended you practice zazen. Unlike other forms of practice, zazen teaches us to practice mindfulness and awareness

at all times. Not only when you are sitting in a half-lotus in your spiritual space. No, according to zazen and the teachings of the Zen masters, you should be meditating at all times. During every action and wherever life may take you. This constant meditation is what the practice of zazen means. This is why Zen is thought to be the type of practice Buddha would have done. Because Buddha didn't only practice mindfulness while sitting and meditating. He was, you could say, totally hardcore, when it came to enlightenment! Would you expect anything less from the Buddha? In fact, according to a lot of the followers of Zen, zazen levels of practice are the only way it is possible to reach enlightenment. It's believed this ambitious state of being can only be gained through constant, daily meditation. Sitting for an hour every day in the half-lotus and trying to focus your thoughts won't cut it, according to zazen philosophy. That's far too "part time" a method of reaching nirvana, according to the Zen masters, and far too half-assed for the disciplined samurai warrior!

Given the difficulties in explaining this profound spiritual practice, we'll confine our explanation to what has already been made clear. All serious Japanophiles are encouraged to study Zen on their own, however. Not only because it is omnipresent in almost all elements of Japanese culture (the references are everywhere, from anime to film to music), but also because this was the religious foundation of the samurai. All Otaku must have a deep respect for the samurai. That's just a basic prerequisite for full membership in the fellowship of Otaku. So, it's advisable to at least understand the basics. The small amount explained here should be enough to provide you with minimum levels of knowledge. However, it's recommended you read some of the essential Zen texts. Most notably, "Shōbōgenzō", written by legendary Japanese Zen master, Eihei Dōgen.

6.4 Samurai Philosophy

In addition to Shinto and Zen Buddhism, there is also a whole genre of writing, in Japan, which was written by famous samurai and warrior philosophers. Although not specific to either religion, the ideas in these works do express the spiritual outlook of the warrior class, which ruled Japan from 1192 AD to 1867 AD. Having been ruled by samurai and shogun warlords, for such a long and

formative span of their history, it is understandable that the philosophies and moral codes of these warriors rubbed off on the entirety of Japanese society, over the course of those 700 years or so. And so, you can't entirely understand the spiritual outlook of Japan, unless you come to know the codes and teachings of the ancient masters. Samurai such as Musashi Miyamoto and Yamamoto Tsunetomo are examples of such samurai masters. They've left great works of warrior philosophy behind, which outline centuries of samurai thought and have, in their wake, infused themselves into the Japanese character.

Although too deep and profound to be related here, we can recommend our other book, "Instruction Manual for the 21st Century Samurai", which was written for exactly that purpose — to put the accumulated wisdom of the samurai masters into a quick reference book, which can be used by the modern samurai to effectively live by the samurai codes. This book is directly based on the teachings left behind by Miyamoto, Tsunetomo and the above-mentioned Zen master, Dōgen. As it's designed to be used for any modern situation — putting the wisdom of the masters at your fingertips, for any modern application, this is by far the quickest way to learn the authentic way of the samurai.

Even if you do not wish to become a modern-day Musashi, you will, at least, gain a clear understanding of these over-arching philosophies, which have become such a part of Japan's spiritual outlook. Although it is not mandatory — which is why we don't describe it, in this book — it is highly recommended that all Otaku make an effort to understand the warrior philosophies of the historical samurai in order to fully understand the traditions, the society and Japanese soul.

7.1 Otaku Community

If you've faithfully applied all the spiritual lessons, which have been outlined in this book, so far, and have taken the previous five commandments to heart, then there is a good chance that you are already a true Japanophile, at heart. You could stand up proud, at any anime convention or Kurosawa film festival, and speak with all the guts and glory of the genuine Master Otaku. You could walk down the streets of Harajuku, itself, and not even draw a stare, from the highly sophisticated Japanese which populate that district. You could stand in the first row at a Swarrrm concert and not even feel remotely intimidated by the insanity — so practiced and polished is your samurai nerve and composure. Now that you have reached these lofty heights, there is only one more lesson to be learned; just one more level boss to set your sights upon, before you can beat the game and log, for all eternity, that high score.

You need community. It is the sixth and last commandment of the Otaku lifestyle. You need to seek out other enlightened Otaku and join together with them into a community. As has been stated, time and time again in this handbook, the true Otaku keeps a respectful distance from genuine Japanese people. They might be delighted if a Japanese person initiates contact, but they won't impose themselves.

Because the true Otaku knows their place and their true spiritual home is in community with others of their kind — with other Japanophiles. It's been too long that Otaku have stood alone, and have hesitated to gather together among their true kindred spirits. And if you truly value the beliefs, the interests and the principles, which define the Otaku lifestyle, then you need to prove your dedication to the Otaku life by joining together with other Japanophiles to build Otaku pride, solidarity and the promotion and continuance of the lifestyle that we all hold so dear.

It is not only my recommendation, to help preserve our culture, it is also your moral duty, as an Otaku, to build community, and the sixth commandment of our chosen path. I, for one, invite you to join my site and social media, through www.samuraicollective.com. Built and designed for all Japanophiles who share my beliefs. Together, we can finally bring the hidden nation of Japanophiles together, at last, to form a cohesive community. And so make the world take heed of our vast numbers, our anime-fueled strength and our mad, ninja-like abilities.

But there are so many more places, where Japanophiles can gather, and so come together, with their own kind, in the spirit of Otaku solidarity. In this chapter, we will list the many ways that we can come together, in a number of venues — from a sushi food festival to a furries convention. There are, literally, hundreds of possible ways you can join together, with others of your kind. So, it should never be impossible for the eager Otaku to fulfill their sixth commandment responsibilities. Only the Weeaboos will intentionally walk alone, harassing genuine Japanese and remaining unaware of the fact that their true place is next to other Japanophiles. As unpleasant as the Weeaboos might be, in the name of solidarity, deal gently with these people. Remember, we were all Weeaboos, at some point, and there but for the grace of Inari goes you. Even the Weeaboo, after all, can be converted to a respectable state of Japanophilia, if shown the error of their ways. Solidarity is your duty, after all, as an Otaku. Under the sixth commandment, you are morally obligated to build strong Japanophile communities. So, take the Weeaboo under your wing (as distasteful as that might be, at first) and try to teach them — maybe lend him or her this

handbook — and so help build our global nation of true Otaku to even greater numbers, through a million converted and ennobled Weeaboos.

To help you reach that honorable goal, we will now share a few tips, in order to help you seek out the Otaku communities near you. And so fulfill the all-important task of finding other Otaku, to join your party — as well as any NPCs, in the best possible tradition of the classic Japanese RPG.

7.2 Otaku Conventions

By far, the best way to find new members for your adventuring party is to attend the many conventions, world-wide, which are designed for Otaku to get together and enjoy all things Japanese. No matter where you live, I guarantee you there is an Otaku convention, of some kind, in your city or in a city near you. We Otaku aren't exactly an endangered species, after all. No, on the contrary — we are legion! If we got together and exerted our might, we could force Bandai Entertainment to get back into the anime business! We're so massive, there's nothing we couldn't do, if we got together. And that's why we so emphatically recommend that you do just that, and get together with other Japanophiles at your anime, manga or classic gaming convention. For me, it is "Ai-Kon Fest", which happens twice a year, here in Winnipeg.

But if you're luckier than I am, and are blessed enough to live somewhere other than Winnipeg — like New York or Los Angeles — then the options available to you are probably infinitely better! As much as I love our Ai-Kon, there are truly epic festivals and conventions out there, which can afford to host millions of Otaku, at a time. Usually these events involve a massive central market place, where manga, anime, video games and paraphernalia, as well as Japanese foods and products are all available for purchase. Usually, there is some form of J-pop or anime music playing, and everyone is cosplaying their favorite anime character. If you don't know what cosplay is, it is the practice of dressing up as anime, manga or Japanese gaming characters. This is usually a big part of the convention and accounts for a lot of the socialization. They will

also have anime-viewings, video game contests (traditionally Super Smash Bros or another team fighting game) and a maid cafe.

Does this sound like heaven on Earth? If so, then congratulations, you have successfully read through this whole book and are now, clearly, a genuine Otaku, worthy of an Otaku identity card, a badge of honor and a matching pair of Katana/Wakizashi swords! Given all these attractions, you can see why we recommend you join your local convention in order to bond with other western Otaku and fulfill your sixth commandment responsibilities. If you are unsure of when and where your local convention or festival takes place, check out the websites in section "8.1 Links" on the next page.

7.3 Otaku Online Communities

If you're not in the mood to go out and socialize, or if, like me, you have to wait six months, between anime conventions, then you can still get out and meet other Otaku, by joining one of the many Otaku-friendly membership sites or following a popular anime reviewer or J-vlogger (a western video blogger who focuses on Japanese topics) and joining in the discussion, within their communities. We've collected a few of the best Otaku websites and the best, most insightful and entertaining anime reviewers and J-vloggers, to get you started on your great Otaku odyssey. Any one of these sites or J-vloggers are a great introduction to the community and we've only chosen those we know are open to their sixth commandment responsibilities and are welcoming to newcomers. Every J-vlogger or reviewer mentioned in the following chapters are easy to find on YouTube or by searching their names, online. At the very least, we highly recommend that you follow or subscribe to their channels, in order to help support the community.

Finding a welcoming community is, indeed, an important point, as we're all Otaku here and we need to learn to get together and support each other. In order to assure that our glorious traditions live on, for future generations to enjoy. So, venture forth, my beloved brethren, put your favorite anime or video game cover song on full blast and burst out into that endless universe of possibilities, which is genuine, glorious and unrepentant Otakuhood!

8.1 Links

www.animenewsnetwork.com - The number one site for getting the latest news on anime, manga and Otaku-related information. Also the main knowledge database for all anime and manga in existence.

www.myanimelist.net - Currently the most popular anime membership site out there. An anime and manga site, where you can chronicle what anime you've watched, manga you've read, and explore what you'd like to watch or read. Completely free, you can easily interact with other members.

www.anime-planet.com - A popular and established anime and manga site, where you can chronicle what anime you've watched, manga you've read, and explore what you'd like to watch or read. Completely free, you can easily interact with other members.

www.gaiaonline.com - A free online membership site, where you can design anime-like avatars and interact with other Otaku.

www.otakubooty.com - A well-established community for Otaku. Providing news, discussions and very open to new members. Membership is free, but limited, unless you pay for full membership.

www.otakuusamagazine.com - Otaku Magazine is the most popular print publication for Otaku news.

www.shonenjump.com - We suggest all Otaku do their duty and help sustain the industry by visiting the page of the legendary Shōnen Jump.

www.theotaku.com - A great place to share fan art or fan comics, this free member site has a pretty decent membership and a forum.

www.cosplay.com - The primary website for the cosplay community. Being one of the pillars of Otakuhood, this free website is a great place to meet like-minded individuals and be initiated into the magic of cosplay.

www.animecons.com - The best site listing anime conventions, including mostly, but not limited, to the United States and Canada.

www.maiotaku.com - the most popular Otaku dating site.

8.2 J-vloggers and reviewers

Misty Chronexia - If you want to know about anime and manga, you need to find a good reviewer. YouTube is full of them, but Misty is my personal favorite. Misty Chronexia is, in fact, a business name, and Chronexia is a male reviewer from Quebec, in Canada. With hundreds of videos of anime reviews and top ten lists, he can quickly give you an idea of what's what, in the anime world. His series reviews are perhaps the most informative and compelling of any I've seen. And so, people who wish to expand their knowledge, beyond the limits of this book, are advised to check out his channel. He also does video game walkthroughs (called "let's plays") on a separate YouTube channel called Misty Chronexia - Octavia.

The Anime Man - Another quality anime reviewer, The Anime Man certainly gets my vote as the most entertaining YouTube reviewer out there. His presentation style is brilliant, his attitude to his audience engaging and his insights on anime are spot on. And, in addition to the anime reviews, he also does the occasional game-related video and information on the Japanese language in his fantastic "Japan 101" series. You can also follow the hilarious animated adventures of the channel's home-made anime mascot. The Anime Man, whose real name is Joey, is based in Australia.

Sharla in Japan - If you want to learn about Japan, itself, you need a genuine J-vlogger. J-vloggers are, generally, defined as video bloggers who are living in Japan and making informative videos about their experiences. There are many J-vloggers out there, these days, but my personal favorite is the popular Youtube channel "Sharla in Japan." With about 350,000 loyal followers, to date, Sharla's channel is an invaluable resource for information on Japan, from a firsthand insider's perspective, and we highly recommend subscribing to her channel. She covers a little bit of everything, from food, culture, events and such Otaku interests as Japanese gaming and cosplaying, in Japan. With over 200 videos, so far, she is well-known as a popular youtuber, both inside and outside of Japan. She has an engaging style and one of my favorite parts of her channel is when she goes out to public events, around Tokyo, and talks to locals. Her channel really gives you a flavor of the ambiance of Tokyo and the local culture and what it would feel like to be visiting it, yourself. Another great aspect of this J-vlogger is that she has strong Otaku interests, herself, including an interest in anime, video games, cosplaying and more -- making her an attractive choice for

Otakus who want to learn more about Japan (or fantasize about visiting Japan) through following her adventures. She works in Tokyo as a translator/content creator, among other things, and is originally from Canada.

Bob Samurai - This is a quality American reviewer who I highly recommend. His series reviews are among the best I've seen, but he is also notable for doing manga reviews as well as a few movie reviews. His excellent presentation style and his overall video quality make his channel an invaluable tool for anyone wanting to educate themselves on anime series. With over 250 videos, to date, and 50,000 followers, his channel is also a welcoming environment for newcomers. For example, Bob Samurai regularly posts "anime discussion" videos that can be a great place for learning from other Otaku, all there is to know about anime and manga.

Digibro - The world of anime reviewers is diverse and varied, and different reviewers focus on different subjects. Apart from anime reviews, American reviewer, Digibro, is exceptional for focusing on other important elements of the anime industry, including definitions of anime and the back-story of the industry, as a whole. He provides well-researched and high quality education on all topics anime-related. A good place to start for a broad education on the anime industry, as well as good quality reviews.

Black Critic Guy (BCG) - Another American reviewer, BCG is another great channel to start with, along your path to anime knowledge. Providing quality insight into a range of anime, he also reviews movies and TV shows. With over 600 videos, there are few series you can't learn about on BCG's channel, so it is a great place to start, if you want to learn more about a variety of series. His style is highly entertaining, articulate and easy to follow, with an engaging and welcoming attitude to subscribers.

BDUB the Anime Master - Our fourth American reviewer, BDUB not only provides high quality anime reviews, but also reviews games and movies. BDUB shares a lot of the good qualities of our other reviewers, including engaging style, informative reviews and high subscriber engagement. In addition, BDUB is exceptional for providing great information about fandom, Otakuhood and the nature of the community.

CharlyJapan - Charly is a French national, living in Tokyo. Although he hasn't been around as long as the other J-vloggers on this list, he is one of my personal faves and is exceptional for vlogging about old Japanese cinema, which is one of his interests -- and is a topic that's difficult to find, among J-vloggers and reviewers. His "2 Minute Japan" video, giving short snapshots into his life, in Tokyo, are easily digested, bite-sized insights of Japan, put in a highly entertaining form. His style is both hilarious and articulate. I recommend Charlie's channel for anyone who wants to learn more about Japanese cinema, snapshots about living in Japan, or who just wants a good laugh!

Overclocked Remix - Not quite a J-vlogger, but still, an addiction to video game music and the many remixes and covers of them, which exist nowadays, is one of the hallmarks of the true Otaku. I have been known to play Super Mario remixes, on my iPod or listen to a guitar compilation of tunes from Revenge of Shinobi, in my car. A lot of these remixes came from Overclocked Remix (OCRE), which is the best YouTube channel, for finding original and high quality remixes of popular video games, spanning from classic NES games to PS4. All serious Otaku are encouraged to check them out and learn the depths of fandom delight, which can come from a well-remixed tune, from among your most cherished video game memories.